FIRST MISSION

The platoon sergeant gave us the lowdown: we were to go in to the eastern side, work up through the infantry, and take the other half of the village under fire.

Once we were safely across the open area, the gunners became spare loaders because the tank commanders were "firing from the hip"—ramming the gun muzzles up to the firing slits of bunkers and blowing them up from the inside. The muzzle blast couldn't be distinguished from the concussion of the warheads. The howl of the turret motors was almost constant. The once stable gun platform became a bucking, heaving monster as the drivers reared up on log and sand fortifications, finishing the destruction with the tracks. Suddenly it was over. I hadn't been in the country for one whole week. . . .

RALPH ZUMBRO enlisted in the army in 1957, trained with the 101st Airborne Division, and spent some time in Germany with the 505th Airborne Battle Group of the 8th Infantry Division. He left the army in 1962 and became an underwater construction worker. He reenlisted specifically to go to Vietnam. A civilian now, he lives with his wife on a ninety-acre farm in the southern Missouri Ozarks.

TANK SERGEANT

RALPH ZUMBRO

POCKET BOOKS

New York   London   Toronto   Sydney   Tokyo

POCKET BOOKS, a division of Simon & Schuster Inc.
1230 Avenue of the Americas, New York, NY 10020

Published by arrangement with Presidio Press
Library of Congress Catalog Card Number: 86-9296

ISBN: 0-671-63945-5

First Pocket Books printing January 1988

10 9 8 7 6 5 4 3 2

POCKET and colophon are trademarks of
Simon & Schuster Inc.

Printed in the U.S.A.

CONTENTS

CONTENTS

6

FOREWORD

Now that the closet has been opened on the agonies of the Vietnam experience, a growing swell of veterans of the era have been committing their experiences to print. There have been a number of superb, insightful chronicles vividly detailing the miseries, the trials, and the personal triumphs and tragedies of the "grunts," the "Thud" and Phantom drivers, and chopper pilots.

The Marines have landed in multiple type faces, and the medics, "spooks," nurses, and even donut dollies have been given their due. The tap on the massive reservoir of the nation's longest war has just begun to flow.

Grunt stories and sagas of aerial combat are great, and deserve every line of prose committed to the sum of their efforts. However, there is one key group of ground-combat elements that has gone virtually unrecognized in mass-circulated writings of the Vietnam experience to date.

That group is Armor and Armored Cavalry—tanks and APCs—those noisy, hot, stinking, giant bull's-eyes that looked oh so good to the grunts when crap hit the fan. Few elements during the Vietnam conflict were used, or misused, more often, in more diverse ways, than were Armor and Cav units.

Ralph Zumbro's narrative provides an old soldier's chronicle of some of the most diverse applications of mounted soldiery in the history of American arms. This book is more specifically a testament to the incredible resourcefulness, the tenacity, the selfless bravery, and the superb adaptability of the men of one U.S. Army, medium-tank company . . . A Company, 1st Battalion, 69th Armor.

Ralph Zumbro epitomized the resourceful, "get-it-done" attitude and persona of the Vietnam-era tanker. During the past eighteen years I often wondered what old sergeant "Zippo" had been doing with the rest of his life. In over twenty years of association with the military, and nearly eighteen in business, I have yet to run across a more mechanically innovative and creative individual. When pure circumstance brought us back into contact, I was tickled to death with his request to write a foreword for his book. Having participated in many of the events so vividly described in these chapters, I can echo his initial fears in relating these combat actions. . . . "They ain't going to believe some of this stuff!"

A solid indicator of the diversity of the mission laid on A Company was its dispersion and attachment to other units operating in Vietnam from the period June 1967 to July 1968. These assignments included attachment to the 3d Brigade, 25th Infantry Division; 3d Brigade, 4th Infantry Division; Headquarters, 1st, 2d, and 3d Brigades, 1st Cavalry Division (Airmobile); 173d Airborne Brigade, the 5th Special Forces Group (A-teams at Plei Mei and Duc Co); and the Republic of Korea Capital Division.

Satelliting armored units meant extended and non-existent lines of supply. Accordingly, armormen had to become masters of field expediency—jury riggers and scroungers. Mine damage, RPGs, and pure attrition forced tankers to be extremely creative when it came to repairs and the requisitioning of parts. The scrounging and field-expedient development activities of Ralph Zumbro alone could fill volumes. Somehow, parts, weapons, and other rare and exotic items, such as food and ammo, always seemed to "turn up" when Sergeant Zippo was on the prowl. As A Company XO, I found his ingenuity invaluable (although I expected a visit from the MPs immediately following any of his sojourns into the unsuspecting supply facilities of any military unit). It didn't matter what it was, Ralph could find it and make it work.

With warped hulls, broken torsion bars, wired-up road-wheel arms, to name just a few of the common maladies, the M48-A3s of Alpha Company and their loving, bitching, ragtag, ball-busting crews established a combat and efficiency record that few similar units could match and none would surpass.

A Company was a unique mix of old soldiers, professionals fighting their second or even third war, and kids, fresh out of AIT. If you weren't a trained "tread head" when you came to us, Alpha would turn you into a top-grade "bullet stabber" in no time. Young buck second lieutenants and Pfc. alike listened, learned, and lived from the guidance of the old soldiers.

Ralph Zumbro's unique, down-home narrative style fits the casual yet all-business combat attitude of A Company. We were all proud of who we were and what we did and could accomplish. Although most of the names here have been changed and not all the detail is clear, the events happened and the men are real. I hope that a good number of the old vets of Alpha Company will read this chronicle. It's for them . . . and by them.

> James F. Walker
> Former Platoon Leader and Executive Officer
> A Company, 1st Battalion, 69th Armor
> July 1967—June 1968

Chapter One

ARRIVAL

When we deplaned at Pleiku Air Base, the first impression was the summer heat and the oppressive humidity—our uniforms stuck to us like bandages. On the deuce-and-a-half ride across the city to Camp Enari (named for a lieutenant killed in one of the Cong's all too efficient ambushes), we got a glimpse of Asian culture. The people were attractive, oval-faced and almond-eyed, smaller in stature than Caucasians and graceful in motion. They welcomed us as guests, instead of as a foreign army. They smiled and waved as the trucks went by, and there was a lot of "Hi, GI," from the kids. The road out of the city and up to the camp gates was a familiar sight to any foreign-duty trooper. All the regular stores had been bought out, and had been replaced with the usual collection of soldier-oriented businesses, each designed to separate a serviceman from his pay as quickly and painlessly as possible.

The camp entrance, however, indicated that all was not sweetness and light. A heavily sandbagged bunker covered each side of the entrance, and armed MPs kept a wary eye on all traffic. Each bunker was equipped with an MG nest, and was part of a barbed-wire bunker line that encircled the post.

The replacement depot was the ordinary work-detail/local-indoctrination operation that we'd all been through. Presently I found myself in a jeep, headed for a tank company. The assignments NCO in the repple-depple hadn't been too encouraging.

"Tank crew, huh? Congratulations, you just became a professional mine detector."

I was a bit nervous.

"You look a little bothered, Sarge," said the supply clerk who had been sent to pick me up, the company's lone replacement.

"I don't know why the repple-depple types seemed to think that all a tank is good for is escorting convoys and checking for freshly-laid mines," I said.

"We've got plenty of time before you're due to report in. How's about a cup of coffee at the PX, and I'll fill you in?" I had learned that one of the first things you do on arriving in a new outfit is get acquainted with the supply and mess people, so off we went.

We settled in at a table underneath a slowly rotating ceiling fan, and he gave me the lowdown. "This is the most scattered company in any army; we're not even legally part of the 4th Division. Sixty-ninth Armor is really part of the 25th Division down at Chu Chi. But the 4th, up here in the highlands, has got a lot of territory to cover, so they asked the 25th to loan them a battalion of heavy armor—and that was us. Then, when the spring monsoon left and the coastal paddy country began drying up, the Air Cav, down on the coast, started running into hardened defenses. They don't have any integral armor so they put out a call for help. General Peers, up here, offered to loan them one company, and shipped us out.''

There was a large map of Indochina painted on one wall of the PX and, as he talked, he pointed to the company's area, gesturing with a half-burnt cigar. ''Pleiku, here, is closer to the DMZ than the Delta, and closer to the Cambode border than the sea. That squiggly red line running east is Highway 19, and our 1st Platoon is responsible for security on the central section of it—the hilly part. The tanks cover a section with their guns, and they're hooked up with the local infantry. It's good duty, in a way,'' he continued. ''They've each got a local following and some girls. Not much action, though, unless you count the occasional mortar bombing, or a VC bridge wrecking.''

Pausing to take a swig of coffee, he said, ''Down the line, past An Khe, the next city is Qui Nhon, one of the ports. When the company moved, the bridges on the coastal highway couldn't take tanks, so they loaded us up on an LCVP, carried us up the coast, and we unloaded over on the beach at Bong Son.''

''So that's where the outfit is now?'' I asked.

''Well, not quite,'' he laughed. ''Bong Son is about seventy-five miles north of Qui Nhon, and Company field base is at Landing Zone [LZ] English, just a bit north of Bong Son proper. Third Platoon is usually somewhere around, but I couldn't guarantee it. Second Platoon is farther out, in a place called An Lao Valley. Those platoons have the most action between 'em; there's something on the radio two or three times a week. Usually it starts with some infantry CO calling for help, and then the tanks call for more ammo.''

"Are we talking about one company of just seventeen tanks?" I exclaimed. "That's a divisional area!"

"You got to understand, Sarge, the 69th are the only jungle-tankers around here, and the 4th says they need the other two companies over on the Cambode border."

Being used to European operations, my next question was, "How do you operate a tank in all that thick brush? I'm trained to hit T-54s at forty-four hundred meters."

"Sarge, I dunno, I'm no tanker, but if you get into one of those maneuver platoons, you'll be wishing that the Army put bayonets on the main guns." I thought he was exaggerating—back then.

Arriving at Company Headquarters, I found a skeleton staff, enough to keep mail and supplies headed in the general direction of field operations. The NCOIC, a staff sergeant, gave me a quick rundown of company organization. He told me how much gear to take to the field—no more than one waterproof bag (you have to be able to carry with one hand and shoot with the other).

"Bunk in here," he said, indicating an empty squad bay. "Pick a clean bunk, haul your excess gear [it was almost everything] over to supply, and they'll get you outfitted with combat equipment."

Yeah, right; I turned in that seventy-five-pound bag of issue uniforms and an optimistic set of civvies. They fixed me up with little more than underwear, socks, poncho and liner, three pairs of fatigues, combat webbing—and a .45 automatic. The supply sergeant advised, "You better pick up a few extra unders, if you intend to keep wearing jockey shorts." At my questioning look, he chuckled, "Guys your size have a laundry problem; you're not much bigger than a Vietnamese, and the mama-sans who do the washing sometimes pinch off a few for their own soldiers. One tanker found a pair of his BVDs on a dead VC."

* * *

Before dawn the next morning, I was driven out to the helicopter field, making sure of two things: first, that I was on the right chopper; second, that the crew chief knew he had a green hand on board.

"Look," he said, "this is normally a milk run, but we have to go in low and drop off mail to a couple of remote LZs before we get to English, so we may take some fire. Can you handle an M60?"

"Sure. I've got full infantry skills, in addition to armor."

"I thought so," he grinned, looking at my parachute badge. "You'll be backup door gunner for this trip." He showed me where the extra ammo cans for the M60 were stored; then he checked his load lashings, muttered something into the intercom, and, with rotors shimmering in the sunrise, we lifted out.

The two bush LZs were just fortified hilltops, but English was a division headquarters, fully as large as Camp Enari. In vain, I scanned for tanks as the chopper settled down.

"I'm assigned to . . ."

But the crew chief cut in. "I don't know a damn thing about this base. The only time I know about an individual company is when it's out in the bush."

I helped them offload, and they lifted out, leaving me standing alone and somewhat bemused on an empty helipad. A jeep drove up and, with some relief, I saw A-1/69 on its bumper. Surprisingly the driver was a 1st sergeant. Tall, lean, and dark, he could have doubled for Rudolph Valentino, except for his southern accent.

"You're Zumbro?"

"Right," I said, handing over my medical records.

"I'm Sergeant Quinton. Hop in. You're going to 3d Platoon. They put in an order for a sergeant/gunner for the 3-4 tank—and you're it. The heavy section moves out in half an hour."

While I was absorbing this jolt, he drove down the taxi lane, dodged a couple of aircraft, cut across the runway, and dropped off the embankment that supported it. Suddenly we were in the sorriest excuse for an armored base that I'd ever seen.

Six tanks were nosed into the embankment below the runway. Three of them were obviously in advanced stages of ordnance-level repair, and the other three were getting ready to move out. I noticed that each one had a giant, mean-looking tiger face painted on its bow and, on each radio antenna, a small black flag bearing a skull and crossbones fluttered gently in the humid breeze.

We were driving down a sloping dusty road, and on the left, past the combat vehicles, a tank retriever and a pair of five-tonners were parked next to a general purpose (GP) tent. Across the road were a field mess tent and another GP with its sides rolled up to expose rows of tables and folding chairs. Vietnamese KPs were cleaning up the remains of breakfast, and the top sergeant spotted me hungrily eyeing the food.

"Go scrounge a quick sandwich from the cooks and I'll send the platoon sergeant over. Nobody ever leaves my company hungry."

The platoon honcho, a mustachioed Georgia boy, folded himself into a chair across from me. "Welcome to 3d," he said. "We're a bit shorthanded now, and about to go bail some infantry out of a hole. We lost our lieutenant last week, so I'm it for the time being. I can't put an inexperienced man in command, you understand. But we're short of tank commanders [TCs], so you've got a choice: either go in under an experienced Sp5 in 3-3 over there, or sit this one out."

"Hell," I said, talking around a mouthful of bacon-and-egg sandwich, "a tanker is a tanker; I'll go in as a loader, if that's what you need."

That seemed to be the right answer and he smiled through his handlebars. "Just between you an' me, I'm checkin' out that boy over there for E6 and his own tank, so how's about usin' some of that gunnery school experience [how the hell did he find out about that?], and give me a report on his turret procedures."

"Sure thing, Sarge."

"Just call me Pappy—everybody else does. Grab yer gear and come meet the crews. We've got to get gone."

I got a little nervous walking up to those combat-hardened professionals, and I could feel ten pairs of eyes measuring me up and down. Pappy gave the introductions and then, stepping back where all the drivers could see him, gave the hand signal to start the engines in all three tanks.

Climbing up on the 3-3 tank, I took note of the name that was stenciled on the gun tube: "Avenger." "She's a good tank," the Sp5 told me. "We're pretty proud of our accuracy." I chucked my bag into the bustle rack and started to climb down into the gunner's seat. "Not yet, Sarge," he said. "We don't have to worry about hostiles around here, and we have an hour's safe ride before we leave the road."

"You mean you don't worry about snipers?"

"Naw, we broke the local VC of that habit months ago, and Pappy keeps us out of rifle range of the hamlets most of the time, until we have to button up and go in."

"How in the hell do you break the sniping habit?"

"Well, only tanks can do it, but put yourself in Charlie's place. What would you do if every time one of your buddies shot at a tank, a 90mm shell and a burst of .50 blew him out of his perch, and white phosphorus and H.E. was indiscriminately tossed into the village?"

"I see what you mean. With that kind of response, there's no future in taking potshots."

By now the small column had left the base entrance

behind, turned north on Highway 1, and was working its way through the small settlement that had grown up around the LZ. The buildings were all straw-thatched wattle and plaster construction, single story dwelling/shop operations. Most were mom-and-pop businesses with living quarters in back and shops in front. When working hours started, they just opened up the front of the living area and put out their wares. This particular group seemed to concentrate on GI services such as laundries, souvenirs, and bars.

The heavy traffic was slowing us down. The streets were clogged with a mix of animal traffic, basket-carrying pedestrians, bicycles, and a popping, sputtering collection of three-wheeled buses. These vehicles, called "ditty wagons," were the bane of high-speed traffic. Underpowered and always overloaded, they were always in the way at the worst possible moment.

"You got to watch 'em," the Sp5 was saying. "If they start to veer to one side, it means they're about to turn the other way."

"But what if you're in a hurrry? How do you get them out of the way?"

"No problem: one burst out of the co-ax* is louder than any horn, and they all head for the ditch. Now watch this. I'm going to use the VC detector." I must have had a blank look on my face, because he explained. "You know how loud the turret motor is? Well, any gook who's been in combat around tanks knows that sound means the turret is hunting for him. Watch that bunch of military-age males over there."

He had been playing with his override lever as he talked, running the hydraulic fluid down, and now the accumulator motor cut in with its usual mechanical shriek. The

---

*Coaxial machine gun.

effect on the four men was astounding—they simply vanished.

"Guilty conscience," the TC said. "Out in the paddies we would either bring them in for interrogation, or send 'em a burst for morale purposes."

The tank platoon section had now cleared the built-up area and we were cruising at a comfortable twenty miles per hour through an emerald green, pastoral countryside. Nothing in that setting seemed more unlikely than war, but there was a column of smoke in the distance, northwest of the road, and I could see helicopters heading for it.

Once we left the road, things began to tighten up. Taking my cue from the rest of the crews, I slid down into the gunner's seat and plugged in the intercom. Cut off from visual contact with the rest of the world, except for the limited view afforded by the sights, I had to depend on what I could glean from the radio for information. A tank platoon communication network is like a party line. Each vehicle has unlimited intercom between its four crew members, and each one, simply by reversing his helmet switch, can transmit over the radios.

These crews weren't playing by stateside or European rules—there was constant chatter among them. It was almost as if the three tanks had been welded together to form one giant machine. In fact, that was exactly what happened when these men learned to fight as a single organism. Each man could be addressed by his name or radio call sign; and the tanks were referred to by name as often as by the more formal military designation. This being 3d Platoon, each call sign was preceded by three and then the number of the individual machine.

In practice, we were not so precise. As we rolled along the rice paddies, there was constant communication.

"Close up, Assassin. Avenger, keep an eye on that grove

over to your right; it's big enough to hide an RPG [antitank rocket] team.''

"Right, Pappy."

And the two tanks obeyed. The commands, however, were obeyed by each crew member. Assassin's driver speeded up without urging from his own TC, and the Avenger's gunner automatically swung his sights to cover the suspected area.

As we approached the village, the sound of sporadic fire began to come in over the intercoms, and the platoon sergeant, in contact with the infantry, gave us the lowdown.

"The infantry was on a routine sweep and they discovered new bunkers in the village complex. When they started to put demolition charges in the bunkers, the whole western half of the village blew up in their faces. There's a tunnel network under the bunkers and now they're all manned and shooting. The infantry don't have anything that can break open armed bunkers so they need fire suppression and can openers. What we're going to do is go in to the eastern side, work up through the infantry, and take the other half of the village under fire. Once we've suppressed small caliber opposition, the infantry will cross the open area and secure the bushes. And then it's business as usual—bust 'em and crush 'em. Remember: shoot up and push down any trees that could hold grenadiers or snipers."

The three tanks halted at the edge of the treeline and a ground guide led each of us to our assigned infantry squad. We moved carefully around the huts and through the fields. As we got into the village proper, the firing picked up steadily; this, I was to learn, was normal when we appeared. Anything that large, noisy, and hostile seemed to attract bullets like a magnet.

To my astonishment, the TCs didn't button up, and the

loaders stood on the floors of the turrets, cradling M3 submachine guns and scanning the treetops for grenadiers and snipers. Even the drivers rode with SMGs on their laps—occasionally a hatch would pop open like a jack-in-the-box and a short burst would zap some hidden menace. I thought to myself, "This is one hell of a sophisticated system."

When we reached our assigned firing positions, we were on one side of a long, open strip of white sand, and the houses and greenery on the other side were sparkling with muzzle flashes. I could see random movement as pajama-clad figures carried ammo and maneuvered for firing position.

A voice came over the intercom. "Keep an eye out for a main gun target, Sarge. I'm gonna probe with the co-ax, but if you see anything that looks good, just flip the switch." The commander traversed slowly, firing careful bursts at suspected and visible targets—even with ten thousand rounds of MG fuel on board, you don't waste it.

Once he'd established to his satisfaction that the immediate area was clear and that our rifle squad knew its business, I started getting fire commands. "Traverse left; see that little clump? Give it a burst. Traverse again, elevate and put a burst in that treetop—it's big enough to hide a couple with grenades."

Christ, I thought. Why doesn't he use the override and put me on target?

He didn't seem disposed to hurry and, being new, I didn't say a word. There was about an hour of this give and take; then, of all things, a scraggly chicken came running down the strip of sand. Some clown took a potshot at it; then one of the tanks gave it a burst of co-ax, and before long it seemed as if the whole damn force was shooting at it. That poor bird was almost hidden in the sand being kicked up around it.

"Goddammit, cease fire!" someone shouted over the radio net and, as we shut down, the infantry also ceased firing. But the dust storm around that harassed bird didn't stop, and it took us a few seconds to figure out what was going on. The VC were shooting at it too.

Pappy never lost his cool. "All loaders, switch to cannister," he ordered. As soon as we'd switched the shells in the nineties, the ground CO ordered a rapid advance which, it turned out, meant full throttle and low gear for us and a dead run for the ground troops. Once we were safely across the open area, the gunners became spare loaders because the TCs were "firing from the hip"—ramming the gun muzzles right up to the firing slits of bunkers and blowing them up from the inside. The muzzle blast couldn't be distinguished from the concussion of the warheads. The howl of the turret motors was almost constant. The once stable gun platform became a bucking, heaving monster as the drivers reared up on log and sand fortifications, finishing the destruction with the tracks. The loaders, quickly exhausted by the heat, the fumes, and the constant shell handling, were put into the useless gunners' seats and the gunners became temporary loaders.

I heard, "Brace yourself," from the TC, and then caught a glimpse of rafters and ridgepole *inside* a house, as the Avenger took a shortcut around a bunker. Suddenly it was over. The bunkers were "busted," all hostile fire had ceased, and the foot soldiers were collecting prisoners and patching up their wounded. I hadn't been in the country for one whole week.

As the infantry continued mopping-up operations, the three tanks pulled out into that contested sandy strip and parked, forming a rough triangle, guns pointed 120 degrees apart.

"We're security for the combat LZ," the Sp5 explained. "Medevac and resupply ships land inside our perimeter and, if things warm up again, we're the rally point.''

The area still needed to be gone over, though, and, not having any riflemen handy, the tank crews dropped a couple of men off each vehicle, leaving the drivers' and commanders' positions manned.

I was elected from the Avenger, teamed with a short-timer, Sp4 Goins, and we circled warily around the tank, searching the scattered bushes for holdouts. This, I learned, was normal for these crews; they trusted neither fate, luck, nor the competence of others. The tankers held their lives in their own hands.

Shortly the battle zone was clear. Choppers began settling in and wounded infantrymen were brought out from the surrounding hamlets. Surprisingly, the stretcher bearers were carrying quite a few civilians who, I was told, would be patched up at English, then brought back home.

Several children were among the evacuees. Pappy explained, ''Brand new orphans. Their fathers are off somewhere fighting and, if the mother gets killed, they come to the medics. See that little girl over there? Her mother warned a squad leader about a house full of VC, and she took a burst of AK slugs meant for him.''

''Well what happened to the VC?'' I asked.

''Full treatment,'' he growled, spitting a streak of tobacco juice. ''Cannister, co-ax, and tracks!''

Back at company base that night, I began learning a new way of life. After supper in the open-air mess hall, I looked around for a barracks tent only to be told that just the permanent headquarters staff had bunkers. The CO, Top Soldier, mess personnel, mechanics, and supply people needed sandbag protection; but anyone who was assigned to a combat vehicle stayed glued to it. Every tank had been issued a heavy tarp and four canvas cots. In addition, each one had small stoves, Coleman lanterns, and mosquito nets. All the tanks carried enough supplies, food, ammo, water, and beer for an extended stay out in the field. The crews sometimes didn't even see this crude company base for weeks at a time. The only reason 3d Platoon was in camp at all was to retrack one section, while the other two tanks of the unit stayed out, working with the infantry, prowling through towns and smashing trails through forests.

When a tank shut down for the night, one of two procedures was used. If there was a reasonable expectation of safety, the tarp was erected. This involved tying one side of it to a track fender and supporting the other side with sections of tent pole. Set up this way, we could be reasonably comfortable; if we had to pull out in a hurry, the tarp was attached with slipknots and one good jerk would allow it to drop over the cots while the tank moved out to deal with whatever had disturbed our well-earned rest.

If the situation was at all iffy, a radically different procedure was followed. The driver adjusted his seat for full recline and slept in position (being careful to keep his head out of the turret space to avoid being decapitated). By fiddling with the adjustment of the tank commander's seat and footrest, it was possible for him to sleep sitting up with his head and forearms resting on the rangefinder. Meanwhile, the gunner could stretch out with his feet hooked on the turret drive motor and his head resting on the TC's footstand. Normally the loader would sleep on the ammo cans that covered the turret floor. Offhand, I'd guess that the average tanker in that company spent about 325 nights in one of these positions during his year of duty.

The reasons for this relatively brutal lifestyle were partly political and partly military. It's not a well-known fact, but it was a tactical reality, that U.S. forces legally were guests of the Saigon government and, as such, we couldn't occupy and hold territory. As a result, any village we cleaned out had to be garrisoned by "indigenous forces," usually local militia, but occasionally regular units of the Army of the Republic of Vietnam (ARVN).

Since the South Vietnamese were spread as thinly as we were and since many of their regiments were under-strength, this doctrine allowed the Cong to reinvest many places. About half the time, a routine patrol would discover a brand new set of combat bunkers in a "pacified area."

Consider this policy along with the fact that the 1st Air Cavalry was fully helicopter-mobile, and had no armored units in its makeup, and you have the makings of a large and hairy problem. Usually the first indication of trouble was an increase in night attacks on villages, or in random snipings, as the local guerrillas got more confident. As mentioned earlier, Company A had developed ways to discourage these rash actions, but the unfortunate ground troops were forced to sit and take it unless they could get the area reclassified as a military objective. What a way to run a war!

Company-size patrols operated on intelligence data from a variety of sources. Sometimes the local villagers would become desperate enough to ask for help, but the most common source of information was the Long Range Reconnaissance Patrols (LRRPs) that both the Viet and U.S. forces sent out.

Information on VC presence was obtained from the Cong themselves. Regardless of propaganda to the contrary, many Cong units were more like bandits than "simple agrarian reformers," and a thief or rustler leaves tracks. The VC were styled as the "night government" of

Vietnam and they would come into a village after dark—with or without the cooperation of the residents.

Under most tactical situations, you just can't sneak around with tanks, but American infantrymen can be very good at night. Many VC units, even up to battalion strength, woke to find themselves trapped by deadly phantoms who materialized out of the night with fixed bayonets.

Typically, on these occasions, we would link up with a company that had been given a suspected region for an objective. In order to fake out Charlie, the task force would make a few halfhearted searches away from the intended target and set up what looked like a temporary camp. Wire might be strung, or mail delivered—anything to make it appear we were going to be in one place for a while.

Depending on the distance to be covered, the ground-pounders would begin moving between the hours of 2400 and 0300. Stacking their packs and heavier gear to be picked up by chopper, they would vanish into the darkness, with their weapons taped to prevent noise, and their faces blackened with camouflage sticks (which, mercifully, also contained bug repellent).

Once we had received word that the foot soldiers were all in place, we'd fire up and go straight for the objective at maximum speed to be able to provide the firepower needed if the situation got out of hand.

This was the normal modus operandi, but there were instances when the shoe was on the other foot, when the tanks were discovered or were jumped by the Cong. Those situations called for some original tactics.

Tanks and infantry usually work as a team in built-up or heavily overgrown terrain, because the heavy guns of the armored vehicles are excellent tools for "breaking and entering," and the foot-pounders can keep antitank teams from getting under the guns and punching a shaped charge through the armor. Theoretically, a buttoned-up combat vehicle is almost helpless in heavy forest or jungle, but there are ways of overcoming this handicap, provided your gonads are up to the strain.

The prime requirement was that we watch each other's tanks, so that if a suicide group tried to hurl a satchel charge into my tracks, that group was taken out by a burst of co-ax from my buddy. If I saw them first, I'd have only two alternatives—heave a tanker's grenade (two pounds of TNT wrapped with barbed wire) over the side, or pivot on the tracks, running one forward and one in reverse, and wrap up the enemy. When the enemy would come out of the overhead growth, attempting to board and capture, the drill was to slam the hatches and let your buddy "scratch your back"—hoping he didn't accidentally riddle the beer cooler. A 1st Platoon tank was once crippled by a mine and then boarded. Not having a "partner," the crew had had to sit it out in a jungle clearing, calling in airburst artillery to clear the VC off the tank's back.

Chapter Two

ON PATROL

When we left company base for patrol, I was sergeant-gunner for Pappy, the platoon sergeant in 3-4, the Ape, which was serving as command tank. The lieutenant who had been their previous officer had been hit in the chest by an antitank rocket while operating the turret with head and shoulders exposed. It was an occupational hazard. The driver was a redheaded Sp4 named Holt, and the loader was Wittlinger. Gradually, I began to blend in with the varied personalities of the platoon, and to learn the ways of this strange kind of war.

The other two tanks in the section were commanded by a pair of E6s. The 3-2, christened Apostle, was under the control of a blond guy who answered to the nickname Rabbit; its driver, "Bronco" Kindred, had been a tunnel rat down south in the Delta. Trained as a tanker, he had been inadvertently assigned to the infantry.

His small stature had made him a natural for tunnel duty and, then a Pfc., he had welcomed the extra pay. He had distinguished himself to the point where the local commander had hung a Bronze Star on him. The general who officiated at the awards ceremony made the mistake of asking the irrepressible Bronco if there was anything he would like. To which he replied, "Yes sir, you can get me out of this goddamn walking-crawling war, and back into tanks where I belong."

S. Sgt. "Pineapple" Watanabe ran 3-5, the A-Go-Go, which had the reputation of setting the best table in the company—when we were in secure encampments and could afford the luxury of decent cooking. Of course, it helped considerably that Wilson, the driver, had been raised in the restaurant business.

These three machines, the Ape, Apostle, and the A-Go-Go, operated as a heavy section, while the other two, the Avenger and Assassin, reinforced by one of the headquarters tanks, worked with the infantry in another area of the Bong Son Plain. Nothing in my training, or in my studies of military history and armored war, had prepared me for the concept of individual tanks operating like knights-errant or horse cavalry charging to the rescue.

The concept of "jungle busting" was also new. Historically, tanks have been most effective in open country, deserts, and plains, or in lightly wooded farm country. The Bong Son Plain was cut up by hilly, jungled areas, and surrounded by green mountains. The plain was roughly triangular, with the apex of the triangle in the north, closed in by converging ridges of mountainous jungle. The southern baseline was formed by the Bong Son River and a range of low hills. LZ English and the city were at the southeast corner of the plain, and LZ Geronimo sat atop the highest point of the eastern ridge.

Company A crews had learned to tear straight into growth so thick that you could see a tank-shaped hole left in the brush behind the hull. Sometimes we'd pass one of these trails later and find that the local Vietnamese had adopted them as permanent roads.

As I learned the ropes and fell into patrol-and-firefight routine, my previous life faded into a dream world. The United States, Pleiku, even company base seemed part of another reality. Here, there was only the brighter-than-reality tropical sun and foliage, the incredibly beautiful land, and a friendly, seemingly peaceful people.

This was the dry period of the year; the rice had been harvested and stored, making the South Vietnamese particularly vulnerable to armed depredations. The Cong had a nasty habit of ripping off the stored food and using it themselves, while blaming the necessity for robbery on the central government.

Two could play at that game, however, and the Saigon government, with the cooperation of high-ranking U.S. military, came up with the idea of confiscating the rice, putting it behind barbed wire, and then doling it out to the villagers. The idea was to keep the farmers fed, but to deny the surplus food to the Cong. So, in addition to searching for VC bases and supply depots, we were expected to become, in effect, finks for the government. They wanted us to go through houses and sound out floors searching for hidden stashes, then report back.

Propaganda planes, twin-engine Cessna Skymasters, crisscrossed the area with loudspeakers, telling the residents what was going on and why. But we still got dark looks when a family's food stash was loaded into an ARVN truck.

After a while, we could determine what areas were safe and which ones were liable to blow up in our faces. For instance, one part of the plain was known as Shangri-la; a patrol there was regarded almost as R&R. On the other hand, the southwestern area was called "VC Valley," and there you treaded lightly, keeping your guard up at all times.

When approaching a new or unfamiliar village, we kept an eye out for the children. They were always eager to see the tanks coming; that meant free candy, recyclable trash, and a chance to trade coconuts and jackfruit for C rations. I guess the grass is always greener on the other side—we couldn't get enough fresh native food and they sought those cans that contained such exotic, foreign delicacies as turkey loaf, pecan cake, and grape jelly. The kids were the key—if there was no greeting party, it meant bad news and we went in with all weapons switched on, ready for trouble.

The farmers were caught in the middle. Sometimes when we went into an inhabited zone, the silence indicated that the VC were not waiting for us, that they had already been there. Sometimes that was harder to bear than combat.

We had to witness the grief of a mother who has just watched her eleven-year-old son being marched off by the Cong for "duty" as a porter on the Ho Chi Minh Trail, or look into the eyes of a father whose daughter has been taken for "reeducation." We saw a teenage girl whose only crime had been selling Coca-Cola and ice to a passing tank—and who had been punished by being shot in the crotch. Her parents brought her to us. Our medic took one glance and started cursing bitterly—working on the child all the while. We called a medevac for her, and our interpreter tried his best to reassure her family.

Some of the villages openly sided with the communists, offering them sanctuary, but many were simply held captive by armed raiders. Sooner or later, though, the tanks would come and, with them, a day of reckoning.

There were usually a few members of the Vietnamese National Police with the infantry, and their aim was to extract as much information as possible from the locals. If a battle had taken place, they would interrogate the prisoners—and I have seen some brutal sights. One captive was strung up by the elbows and flogged on the testicles. Another was held down while a rawhide thong was tightened around his skull, compressing the bones. The policeman then popped him on the head with a little mallet, causing a ringing in his cranium.

Occasionally the interrogation and the battle swapped around. The VC would lay low, counting on the innocent-appearing villagers to cover for them. The procedure then was a bit different. More policemen were flown in, and the people were rounded up for the magistrate to count heads. If any great number of known males of military age could not be accounted for, the police would get nasty with the civilians. Frequently the young men were only hiding in the bomb shelters to avoid the draft and the proceedings came to a peaceful end.

The bomb-proof shelters generally were allowed by the authorities, as long as they contained no firing slits and no false floors. The normal construction was a series of coconut-palm logs stacked in a row of A-frames with double ridgepoles. Over this, a layer of clay was laid and then hardened with fire. Last, a few feet of sand were heaped over the composite, resulting in a crude, loaf-shaped structure which could withstand heavy bombardment.

The bunkers could hide more than draft dodgers. On one occasion, after some back-and-forth between the fuzz and whoever was in a bunker, it was determined that the inhabitants would not come out. The Viet commander asked Pappy to open it up gently, if possible.

Using tracks and dead weight, Holt put the Ape on top of the structure and began a slow rotation. This was a standard tactic with us and the drivers were all expert enough to balance fifty-two tons and eight-hundred horsepower on top of the ridgepoles. Slowly, as the tank ground its way down, the logs, like the bones of a dead animal, began to emerge, driven out by the tracks.

Suddenly, four Cong squirted out, firing as they ran. False fronts fell from other bunkers and automatic weapons began stuttering. Infantry and police started falling and the ping-whee of ricocheting bullets filled the air around the tanks. I had been perched on the turret with the loader and, at the first burst, I slid into the gunner's seat. Holt backed off the mound of rubble and, as the infantry tried to get organized, 3d Platoon went to work like a well-oiled machine.

By now I'd acquired a combat nickname, and Pappy cut in with it on the intercom. "Those two bunkers, Zippo," he said, whipping the turret with his override.

"Yeah, I see them, between the house and the buffalo pen."

No more commands were needed; the 90mm barked twice and an armor piercing (AP), followed by a high-explosive plastic (H.E.P.), opened that can of worms. With another pair, the second fortification was silenced. The technique first annihilated the occupants, then covered the hole with debris.

"Nice work, Zippo," someone wisecracked from another tank. "Kill 'em and bury 'em in one operation."

A heavy automatic opened up from a well-camouflaged position between two houses, and I caught a glimpse of the Apostle heading for it—preaching fire and brimstone. Unexpectedly, my controls went dead as the

TC grabbed the override, and the co-ax began a snarling song of death. Pappy, having spotted a group in the open, was hip-shooting, using the tracers to mark his stream of fire.

"Cannister," he commanded. I flipped the main-gun switch and set the ranging computer for point-blank fire. The turret became a swirling hell of ammonia-tainted smoke and flying metal as Wittlinger, stripped to the waist and sweating rivers, fed the 90mm. Half the time, I couldn't tell what was going on since my view was restricted to the sights.

Periodically, though, Pappy could spare the time to give us a briefing and, since the Ape was a command tank, we had the extra radios and could hear what was going on over the command net. This time we had been caught flat-footed. The Cong had been under the town and were able to call for reinforcements. Many of the houses had fully-developed combat bunkers beneath them, so the place was literally swarming with hostiles. Desperately we backed, filled, and fired, trying to make sense of the muddle.

Gradually a pattern emerged. The village was one giant ring of well-concealed fortifications, and we had gotten inside it. Most of its firing positions faced outward so full firepower couldn't be brought to bear on us. It could, however, be used to prevent reinforcements from reaching us. The extra companies that had been flown in were pinned by the fire of interlocking bunkers. If there was any rescuing to be done, A Company would have to do it. We could get some help from artillery, but those bunkers were tough.

Pappy and the ground CO got together and decided to concentrate on one point in the ring of bunkers. At this point, we got the welcome news that help was on the way in the form of our headquarters tank section—the two machines that were the company "reserve." The 6-tank commanded by Cheyenne Black, who was an experienced close-combat fighter, and the dozer tank, Executioner, bossed by Sergeant Hiemes, specialized in bunker-busting. They had been working with the other section of our platoon up in the north end of the plain and had been headed for Bong Son for some light repairs when the shit had hit the fan. Captain Williams, our company commander, diverted them when he got the word that three of his protégés were in trouble.

By now we were running low on ammo. I traded jobs with Wittlinger who, nearly exhausted, was resting in my gunner's seat. The exhaust blower was on at full blast but it wasn't helping much because the turret was buttoned up. We had been boarded, and had almost got a grenade down the hatch before Pappy got the lid shut. Old "Guns A-Go-Go" had given us a back-scratching but we were still reluctant to open up.

"Chopper 3-4, this is 6-Alpha," came Black's welcome, gravelly voice over the radio. "Where can we do the most damage?"

"Have you got the can opener with you?"

"That's roger," came Hiemes's clipped voice. "We got a new hydraulic pump and the blade is working fine."

The infantry CO cut into the conversation, "We're about halfway down their throat; if we can kick their teeth out from the inside, can you break a hole in that bunker ring?"

"Sho-nuf. Just tell us where to hit."

They conferred a while longer, and then called back to artillery for a little white phosphorus and smoke on the eastern edge of the ring. As the smoke descended, the ground troops faded back into cover—they had no business in the unbridled hell that was to follow.

We had by now opened up the top hatches to have a

breather before the blast, and I got a quick look at the town. The once neat, clean village was a shambles. Almost every house, hut, and barn was in flames, the residents nowhere in sight. Pigs, chickens, and cattle were running everywhere, and a lone water buffalo wandered aimlessly.

Moving nervously into the brush, feeling naked without our infantry sidekicks, we eased up to the rear of the defensive line, punching out our remaining cannister shells as we went, trying to flush RPG teams before they got in under our guns. We fed H.E. and H.E.P. into the back of a trio of bunkers and hosed their sides with co-ax, driving the antitank teams into the open where Black's guns could work on them.

Then the bunker next to the three we had assaulted began to change shape and, suddenly, a dozer blade emerged—followed by the turret and hull of the Executioner. The flaming red "Crown 7" painted on her was a welcome sight. The old girl was living up to her name as the turret, swung sideways to the line of travel, spit a continuous wall of flame and lead.

We had been tired for so long that the speed of a fresh crew was like a miracle. Cheyenne Black was trailing to the dozer's right rear and, as Hiemes's hull cleared the end of the opened log fortification, the 6-tank inserted a pair of H.E. shells into it—and that was that. The dozer swung left, dropping a body off the top of its blade as it jerked through the turn, and dug into the next obstacle.

They worked as a team, the blade tank opening the ends of the sand-and-log forts and its running mate pulverizing the occupants. There had been a World War I–type trench works between the bunkers and, as Assassin and A-Go-Go went out to reammo, we fell in behind the wrecking crew, straddled the trench, and went back to work. Holt followed the zigzag line and, bleary-eyed from smoke and fatigue, I stared through the grimy sights, putting short bursts into ghostly shapes and barely-seen movements.

By the time we opened a gap for the relieving infantry the Ape had almost run dry, so we withdrew to a helicopter-delivery ammo point to refill our shell racks. Twice that day and once during the night we had to pull back to replenish our ammo supplies.

We kept prowling through the desolate, blasted wreckage far into the night, moving by infrared headlights, sabering the tropic darkness with multimillion-candlepower xenon searchlights. No one could count the groups of VC who, speared by a light beam, were then smashed to pulp by cannister shells—thirteen hundred metal cylinders from a disintegrating 90mm warhead.

The tanks' lights were aided by multihued parachute flares from orbiting dragon ships, and star shells from artillery. One by one, the last pockets of resistance were cleared up, and at about midnight we finally began to move out. We'd been fighting for twenty hours from the moment Holt had first started to open that bunker.

The Cong had thought they were going to spring a trap on the old pros, and it had backfired—costing them a base camp and huge amounts of men and supplies. It took a week of digging, crawling, and blasting to finish obliterating the underground works. By that time, 3d was ready for a rest. We almost got one.

After the last of that underground supply depot had been blown and the infantry airlifted out, Captain Williams flew out to make a final equipment inspection and check out his troopers. Company base was at English but the CO seemed to spend more time in the air than did most pilots. Division Command had assigned him his own personal gunship as transportation and he'd been known to wade right into a firefight, rather than just sit on top and supervise. But now he sounded a bit harried as he conferred with the platoon sergeant.

Normally, the Old Man was as protective as a mother hen about the health and well-being of his men and tanks—but he had a monkey on his back. A regular infantry division has one tank battalion and one armored cavalry battalion in its makeup—in other words, about 125 iron murder machines. The Air Cav had none, and our pitiful seventeen were trying to support the whole division. Trying? Hell, we were doing it!

That worried, half-apologetic tone in the Old Man's voice meant we weren't going to be able to relax just yet. "Tell you what, Sarge," he said. "You need a little rest after this, so I've got a special detail for you." He dug a map out of his case and Holt, perched up on the Ape's turret, read off its numbers to the rest of us plugged into the tank's intercom—the electronic grapevine again. We knew even before we'd been briefed that we were getting coastal duty.

"The Old Man's picked out a sweetheart for us," Pappy said, and we looked knowingly at each other as the captain's chopper faded into the distance. "This section of beach and hills never has been adequately patrolled, and there's a regular seaborne Ho Chi Minh Trail coming down the coast. There's a string of islands that protects the smugglers' sampans from destroyers and gunboats—but not from us. The gooks have never seen us working at long range, so the presence of tanks probably won't make them too cautious and we may bag a few. In the meantime, there's a beautiful beach with six-foot surf, and the sea wind is bound to be cooler than these paddies. We're supposed to get a couple of weeks of this till 2d Platoon can be turned loose from An Lao Valley."

"Aw, come on Pappy," one of the gunners kidded. "Everybody knows there's really no 2d Platoon. That's just a line of bullshit to convince us we're not the only tanks in Vietnam.''

"There is too," the platoon honcho exclaimed. "I heard Hazelip on the radio only a week ago."

"Well, I guess there must be at that," the gunner admitted. "Ol' Sergeant Death is just too mean to get killed."

With a wave of good-natured hilarity and with expectations of surf and sleep, we mounted up and headed for the highway—and, hopefully, the beach.

Chapter Three

ACROSS THE PLAINS

With anticipation running high, we pulled out of that wrecked village and headed east—only to run into a desolate, uninhabited area infested with track-breaking mines. Since the lead tank took the brunt of the damage, we rotated the job to keep the strain from demoralizing one crew. We'd hit three mines in less than two days. Now it was the Ape's turn again. Holt had no sooner buttoned up and moved us into the lead position when a jolting concussion tore three sections off the right track.

"Goddammit, are we *ever* gonna get clear of this blasted plain? This is the . . ."

"Cool it, Holt," Pappy ordered. "You know we're only a few miles from the hardtop."

"Okay, okay, if it's gotta be that way. But this is one huge minefield."

"Right, and this tank can't fly so the only way out is overland. Now let's get to work."

As near as we could figure out, the VC must have intended secretly to fortify the entire area—before we scragged their headquarters and blew their tactical reserve sky-high. Most of the hamlets were virtually depopulated, and no matter where we turned we seemed to hit those mines, even in heavy forest.

Now, with the ease of long practice, we set about repairing damage from the last explosion. First, with another tank close by acting as a shield, we dug out the embedded dirt and rocks. We had long since learned to work as a team. As one man spun the end-connector bolts loose and dumped the damaged track blocks, another hooked up the jacks while I disconnected the spare track sections from where they hung on the turret rail. Half an hour after the explosion, we were on the move again.

This place was one large booby trap, and the only way you could jump off the tank safely was to land in the tracks we had just made. Even our shotgun-riding infantry wasn't safe; several of them had been nailed by punji stakes—three-foot slivers of fire-hardened bamboo, placed in the ground at odd angles all through and around the abandoned villages.

We never did figure that out. There was no record of any battle, and the damage didn't look as if anything heavy had been used. It was weird—no people, few animals, antitank mines all over, but the village food stashes hadn't been ripped off. In one hootch I found a lonely caged bird that, when set free, adopted me. Naturally, he was named Charlie.

Eventually we got clear of that mess and were back up on the hardtop of Highway 1. The Avenger and Assassin were due to join us, and they were having the same hard time we had just had. So we set up not far from a little market town and waited for them, taking the opportunity to get some laundry done and to get haircuts.

This was a new one on me, but the guys explained. "The main roads are the truck and bus routes," Holt said, "and the farmers bring their salable produce and livestock in. You notice the hamlets aren't plugged into a road network?" Now that he mentioned it, I realized that the only communication that existed off the main roads were the paths on top of the paddy dikes.

"Right," Wilson said. "So these little towns buy the produce or serve as collection points for whoever does the buying."

"When they find out we're staying overnight, what's the chance of a hit?" I asked.

"That's been tried," Watanabe said with that dry humor of his. "They've learned the hard way that these 'tiger-face' tanks are best left alone. They never know when one of them will take a notion to blow something up."

He was referring to the M79 grenade gun each one carried. We had developed the habit of lobbing 40mm shells out at odd intervals during the night. That, plus the occasional burst of MG fire into the nearest bushes, generally assured a reasonably peaceful sleep. Also, at that time, I think the VC didn't know about our seventy-five-million-candlepower infrared searchlights and the sights that went with them.

As the guys were assuring me that this was a normal operation, a couple of middle-aged women came up on bikes. "You stay long GI?" Watanabe and Rabbit launched into a half-English and half-Viet conversation and, before long, the women took off, all smiles. About thirty minutes later, a small fleet of girls on bicycles showed up, some with empty baskets for our laundry, some carrying loads of Coke, beer, and ice. Once we had restocked the "necessities,'' Pappy turned part of each crew loose for a few hours in town.

I experienced a Vietnamese haircut. The barbershop is more than a mom-and-pop operation; it's a cottage industry. Everyone gets into the act. The shop is in open air on the front porch of a street-level, thatched cabin. The first thing they do is sit you in a low, padded chair. Next come the steaming towels that most of us have never seen except in old movies. Then, when your hands are taken, you learn that the kids are in on this too, to give you a manicure. When the heat has softened the stubble, out comes the shaving mug and the straight razor—and the three-day shadow vanishes. But what gives with those half-inch mini-razors? You soon find out, as they trim the hairs in your ears and nose. Meanwhile, the kids, having finished with your hands, remove the dust-caked jungle boots and apply hot cloths to your tired feet. If these folks opened up shop in the U.S., I thought, they'd have to sell franchises to keep up with demand.

The haircut over, papa-san inquires if I want a massage. After the last couple of weeks jolting around in the Ape's turret, that's a definite affirmative, and I get stretched out on a thin mattress. The masseuse is a seventy-five-pound girl who takes off her sandals and walks delicately up and down my spine, digging in with her toes—strange method, but it works. I rejoin my buddies, mentally converting the cost in piasters, and get another shock—it had cost only fifty cents American. As we walk the streets, I happen to glance down—someone had given my boots a buffing.

In this culture, much of the work seems to be done in the open. A group of ropemakers are twisting a ship hawser in the street, some of them deftly feeding coconut-husk fibers into the skein, while others twist the strands into a coil three inches in diameter. Down one alley, we hear the sound of sawing, and see an old-fashioned sawpit converting logs to lumber that is then loaded onto a waiting bullock cart. Small, open-air restaurants serve delicious, but mysterious food. (Rule one when eating Vietnamese cuisine: don't ever ask what the meat is—it could be snake, dog, or monkey.)

We all agree that communism wouldn't suit these people at all; everyone seems to be a natural capitalist. You can't walk a dozen steps without tripping over a salesman. Even those with nothing to sell had rented their porches to some enterprising entrepreneur. We could find nearly everything the crews needed, except fuel and ammo. One man even had a dented, but unopened, case of C rations for sale.

"I see why company base is a bit crude," I said to Holt.

"Yeah, we live on the local economy most of the time. The only thing we need from base is fuel, ammo, and mail—and that comes in by air. The local infantry company honcho orders tank supplies from Division, and we don't see English for weeks or a month; so we're just about on our own out here. The people are so glad to see the Cong losing—most of 'em anyway—that they fall all over themselves trying to be helpful. If any mines get planted tonight, some old mama-san will slip out before dawn and put bamboo markers over them."

"He's right," Wilson agreed. "They know from relatives up north that life under Uncle Ho is no picnic. Besides, they're realists; they'll stick with the winning side. Back in '65, the North Viets slipped a couple of divisions through Cambodia and the Air Cav shot the nuts off 'em up in the Ia Drang Valley."

"Yeah," Holt said. "We've got the buggers on the run. Why the brass doesn't finish it up, I don't know, but if they said, 'get on line and head north,' I'd re-up right now!"

After the other two tank crews finished their shopping, we rolled on up the highway, dropped off our infantry at

a small, ARVN-manned LZ, and drove out to open country, headed for the coast. This was paddy country, and
Holt had to be careful to avoid getting buried to the fenders. These drivers were actually heavy-equipment artists;
getting stuck was embarrassing to them. And because the
tank that pulled you out usually charged a case of beer for
the service, a clumsy driver wasn't popular.

The turns were the weak point; treads put less pressure
on the ground than would a man's boots, but a turn dragged
them sideways, breaking through the surface. A flooded
paddy is very soft and virtually bottomless.

The trick was to go straight and fast across the wet dirt,
aiming for a solid spot for turns or stopping places. So
Holt would pick out a hamlet mound or a clump of woods
in the distance, and shoot across at better than thirty miles
per hour. If we needed to turn or stop before reaching the
hard spot, the next best thing was the intersection between
two dikes, with the tracks perched on the ''X.'' The high
conduits also could support the weight for a while. These
double walls of earth had water troughs cut in them, and
served to move water from holding ponds to remote paddies.

Once we crossed the lowlands, all we had to do was
climb the coastal hills and there it was—the South China
Sea—turned red by the sunset and rimmed with beaches.
From up on the ridgeline, we could see why the patrol
boats had problems. The shore was protected by a string
of rocky islands, and the sea was cut into myriad tricky
channels and sand bars. My own experience as a yacht
captain and tugboat helmsman in Florida told me that those
sand-choked channels would be changing continually—
even between tides.

''Choice Shopper 3-4, this is Nautilus 6. Do you hear
me? Over.''

"This is Chopper 3-4 Delta [the Delta identified which crewman was talking], I have you loud and clear, wait one. Hey Pappy, the Navy's on the horn again."

A hand emerged from the bustle rack, where our honcho was resting after his spell of night watch, and drew the intercom helmet into the blankets. "This is 3-4, what can we do for you?"

"We have a group of six motor sampans working down the inshore channel," the patrol-boat skipper said. "They're out of range of our 81s, and should be about two thousand yards from you. Do you think you can hit them?"

"Easy," Pappy answered. "Can you give me a rough bearing?"

As the Navy fed information to us, we got the tanks out of our defensive laager (circular night formation) and lined up on the beach. All the searchlights were on infrared so as not to startle our intended victims.

Sergeant Bell, six-and-a-half-feet tall and the Avenger's boss, picked them out first. "Bearing 055, they're just about to cross between us and that little island."

"OK, I got 'em," and other affirmations came from the TCs, as the turrets quit hunting and swung to the new bearing. All engines were ticking over slowly, powering the searchlights. Our TC gave quick instructions.

"When I give the word, I want those beams on white light. Override—shoot from the gunner's positions."

"Roger."

"Now!" the TC snapped, and five blue-white beams with three-quarters of a billion candlepower came on like an artificial sun. Scant seconds later, the commanders had spun the rangefinders and the 90s went off in a ragged volley.

"Take the straggler, Zippo."

As Wittlinger dropped another H.E. into the breech, I set the cross hairs on the wildly dodging sampan. We weren't the only ones trying for a double kill; five more tracers flashed down the beams and converged on the hapless smuggler. Where there had been a small fleet, there was now rapidly sinking wreckage.

"Shopper 3-4, this is Nautilus. That was some shooting! What have you got on that beach anyway? You looked just like a light cruiser opening up."

"Nautilus, this is 3-4—just a platoon of main battle tanks is all."

"Well, welcome to the squadron. We've enjoyed doing business with you. Nautilus out."

"Roger that. Good hunting. Shopper 3-4 out."

We had been on the beach for about a week, thoroughly enjoying ourselves. During the day, we pulled much-needed maintenance on the tracks, body-surfed in luke-warm seawater, and played softball in the dunes and tag with the local kids. There were two fishing villages within easy walking distance of our position—picturesque groups of thatched beach houses with fishing sampans drawn up to them. Like most of the Vietnamese, the people here were friendly and willing to sell or barter fish. We had several fish fries—Hawaiian style—with the A-Go-Go officiating.

Then the war found us again. For quite a few nights, we had been holding random conversations with passing patrol boats but nothing had come within range of our guns until this night—which also turned out to be our last one on the beach.

We were sniped at only once, but the incident caught us with only the day guards posted in the turrets, while the rest of us played in the surf. As the bullet pinged off the armor, the man blurted the first thing that came to mind. He shouted, "Surf's up!" then, "Sniper!" We were literally caught with our pants down. Fortunately it wasn't serious, but I got back to the Ape wearing a pair of skivvies and a pistol belt. By then, the sniper had already been taken out with H.E. through the bush where he was hiding. But the impromptu warning stuck with the platoon. From then on, the words "surf's up" would serve to put us on alert.

In the morning, word came over the radio. "3-4, this is Chopper 6. Our second element is in place south of you. Break up your position and proceed to ———." He gave a string of numbers that most of the crews had apparently committed to memory.

"Geronimo again," one man bitched. "I knew it was too good to last."

"It could be worse," Pappy said. "At least Geronimo is sniper-proof, and the infantry handles night watch so we'll only have to keep one turret hot. Also, I hear they got a new cook."

"Now, that is good news," Rabbit said as he swung up on his turret. "The last one was a refugee from a hog farm."

"Okay, move out, line formation," Pappy said, "and keep those gunners scanning. We've got a lot of territory to cover before we get to paddy country."

Chapter Four

GERONIMO

We crossed the coastal hill chain just north of LZ English, ran up Highway 1 for about twenty miles, and then, skirting the base of the eastern range, drove out onto the lush farmland of the Bong Son Plain.

Firebase Geronimo, perched on a windy mountaintop almost at the northern end of the plain, was intended to be an unreachable fortress in the sky. It had been set up entirely by heavy-lift helicopters. Artillery, supplies, even water had been brought in by air. The plan had been for chopper-riding infantry to descend like swooping hawks on hapless VC that the recon patrols turned up.

Actually, the heavily fortified villages, equivalent to our strategic hamlets, stopped them cold. The tunnel-connected, World War I–style bunkers, manned by machine gunners with interlocking fire zones, could be overcome only by heavy bombardment or tanks. Since air or artillery attack would have destroyed the villages they wanted to liberate, the Air Cav elected to use heavy armor for forcible entry. When A Company had first arrived in the operational area in late 1966, the forces from LZs English and Geronimo had been locked in stalemate with the local VC.

Third Platoon, drawing the northern segment of the plain as its assignment, had immediately broken the deadlock. Operating in pairs, the tanks had assaulted the defensive rings and opened them up like sardine cans, allowing the infantry access to the interior of the settlements.

The technique was an instant success, but the armormen had had a problem. Their company base at English was two days away cross-country, so they had had to rely on aerial supply. Worse yet, while the infantry could rest in a secure mountaintop haven, the tanks had had to sweat out nights on the plain.

The dilemma was solved when Sergeant Hiemes and the dozer tank were assigned to the platoon to allow it to split into three pairs. Both Tank Commander Hiemes and the driver had been heavy-equipment operators in civilian life, and they made short work of that hillside, cutting a one-tank-wide, engine-straining trail up the steep grade.

Now, almost a year later, as we approached the base of the ridge dominated by the LZ, the trail looked more like a pencil mark on a wall than a road. As we took the grade, there was a sharp drop on one side and an almost vertical rise on the other. After several heart-stopping turns, we lurched over the last hump and Geronimo opened up to view.

The first impressions were of dust, sky, and distance. Feet, wheels, and tracks had long since shredded the last of the original vegetation and pulverized the dirt to a fine, all-pervading powder. There was a lookout tower on the crest of the hill, and from there you could see the South China Sea in the east, and nearly to the highlands in the west.

Supply was still by helicopter (Sergeant Bell called them "heligoflipters" and the word still comes up in my memory today), and each delivery created a dust storm of monumental size—leaving everything covered with a fine coat of grit.

Rumor had been correct about the mess facilities. The infantry and the howitzer battery who shared the base had combined their cooks into a battalion-sized mess, and the food was superb.

The platoon had split duties; one section was always on the hill acting as direct-fire artillery, while the other was out beating the bushes looking for Charlie. The 105mm howitzers could support the Area of Operation (AO), but our pinpoint capability was needed desperately. Our 90mm, initially designed as an antiaircraft gun, can hit an individual soldier at two miles.

Every evening the crews on artillery assignment would set up for H&I missions (harassment and interdiction). The idea was to use our range-finding and target-fixing ability to acquire targets in the daytime, without actually firing on them. Then at night, we would return to the sight settings with our internal controls and fire shots at unpredictable intervals—in other words, when we damn well felt like it. We learned from captured VC that they didn't like this method at all, because we were shooting at the trails and passes they used for resupply and movement.

On one occasion, working with the infantry, one of the squad leaders told Pappy that a certain village was building combat bunkers with firing slits. Bomb shelters were okay, but firing slits were a definite no-no; so we decided to straighten out that particular group. Just before dark, three tanks sighted in on the individual bunkers with a range of about thirty-five hundred yards. Then we sat back and waited for full darkness. At about 2300, we popped a few into the general area, driving the Cong into the bunkers. After giving them time to get settled, we switched over to precision controls and dropped H.E. delayed-firing shells into the individual fortifications.

The next day, when we came down off the hill, the infantry CO made it a point to check that village over thoroughly—and there was wailing and gnashing of teeth. They had the bodies laid out—all military-age males. Apparently the men had thought that we were preparing for a night attack and had manned the bunkers in expectation, leaving the noncombatants outside. Our precision gunnery had reduced the fortifications without damaging the rest of the town. I don't think anything except tanks can be that selective. I have personally smashed a combat position without damaging the house or livestock beside it.

The fact that we couldn't legally hold land we had won created an extremely weird situation. We had to drive out of that town knowing damn well another group of VC would move in at any time, even against the wishes of the inhabitants. There simply weren't enough ARVN to go around and, sooner or later, we'd have to clean it out again.

As we roamed the plain, the veterans pointed out the scenes of previous battles to us newcomers. Many times, as a pair of tanks and an infantry unit entered a village, the crews already knew the layout, having fought there before. Several days after the night bombardment episode, we'd been hooked up with a company of grunts and sent on a week-long sweep, working down the west side of the valley. The mission was to check old combat sites for signs of reinfestation and to destroy any new military construction.

When the paddies and fields were dry, the tanks had full mobility, and things went a lot faster than night operations. Rather than having to wait while the riflemen skulked through wet paddies, we could simply load them up and take off. When a section of tanks, each carrying a couple of squads of infantry, comes charging in at thirty-five miles per hour, there isn't much time for the enemy to get ready.

I remember one village, a really beautiful place. It was built on a rise at the edge of a large forested hill; a small stream ran through it, and the houses were set among groves of trees—almost as if they had been landscaped. Ape was in the center, with Avenger and A-Go-Go on the flanks. The drivers slowed as we neared the hedgeline, and our infantry dropped off the tanks, hit the ground running, and formed a skirmish line.

"Hey Sarge," Holt said over the intercom. "Ain't this the village where we took all that mine damage last February?"

"Yeah, I've already warned the infantry CO. Now pipe down, button up, and keep your eyes peeled."

Switching his helmet mike over to radio transmit, he reminded the other two TCs, "Stick close to fruit trees; push 'em down if necessary. Charlie doesn't usually plant mines next to crop trees. Keep looking into the trees, though—there were a lot of snipers in them last time."

"I remember," Watanabe came back. "We had to disassemble that schoolhouse piece by piece. . . . Hey, no kids. I think this place is hot!"

By now I was in the gunner's seat, and Wittlinger, head just barely poking out of his hatch, was searching the trees with binoculars, a submachine gun hanging across his chest.

"Er . . . Sarge," he said, interrupting the radio conversation.

"Yeah Witt?"

"That water buffalo's got an extra pair of legs."

Pappy used the override, swinging the turret, and I laid the sights on the offending animal. The extra feet wore tire-tread sandals; a VC was trying to use the beast as cover while he sneaked across an open space between buildings.

"Try not to hit the buffalo," Pappy said. "After all, it *is* someone's work animal."

Shifting the cross hairs slightly, I put a short, one-tracer burst behind the critter—which promptly took off, leaving a rifle-toting native to receive the next one. The infantry had already gone to ground, and we waited apprehensively for more action. The place had gone deathly still after the last echoes of machine-gun fire faded away, and we were all expecting it to blow up any second.

A rocket flashed out from behind a house and slammed into our bow, gouging the armor but not penetrating. Witt and I punched back a pair of nineties and the dwelling caught fire. An MG opened up from a patch of brush, and Pappy, now busy with the radio and a pair of riflemen, said curtly, "Take 'im, Holt." The driver, long since buttoned up and steering by periscope, rammed the Ape's bow straight into the MG, crushing it and the gunner.

Avenger, one hundred yards to our right with another pair of squads, reported no response and, after that little spat, all we could see were a few dim figures swiftly vanishing into the distance. The VC, apparently too few to fight effectively, had decided to retreat, and had left a small holding force to give the main body time to get clear. Our infantry, probing carefully, flitting from cover to concealment, soon established that the place was safe. A-Go-Go remounted his riflemen and made a dash through the hamlet. He reported no contact on the other side either.

Once the "all clear" was given, we began rounding up the locals for interrogation by the National Police, who were flown in from English. There were only six squads of infantry with us, that being all we could carry. The rest of the company was being airlifted in from the last village.

This was a war of incredible extremes. As the adults were rounded up, kids came out of the woodwork, and soon the Ape, its hull hot and smoking from combat, was surrounded by a horde of children. They wanted candy, C rations, and scrap metal; and shortly, the boys were climbing trees for coconuts, breadfruit, and mangoes to barter with us.

Normally, after one of these bust-ups, we would move several miles for night laager—for safety's sake. On no account would we ever sleep where we'd fought, and we *never* stayed twice in the same place. One-night stands were the rule. Brigade command had other ideas about this one, though, since they had reports of other contacts in this general area. Thinking they were on the trail of a large force, the command decided to consolidate some of its scattered search parties. We got the word that Apostle and Assassin were escorting another company of grunts into the area.

Dusk was approaching, but when Pappy requested permission to pull out and laager up in the open, he was bluntly informed that this settlement was going to be headquarters for a large sweep, that the tanks would be given places in a combined perimeter. Since we had no officer of our own to intercede, we were stuck.

The first night wasn't bad, with about 350 infantrymen around, but the following day they started splitting up. The platoons went out in pairs, searching according to a preset plan, taking the hamlets in order. We rode out with them and helped in the searches, but that night we were pulled back to the command post. This made two nights in a row, in a place where we never should have stayed once.

By the end of the third day, we were very apprehensive, expecting bad news. Since this was primarily a search-and-destroy mission, there were some engineer mine-detector crews with us, and that night we had the teams sweep the tank positions for surprises. Sure enough, they found a heavy charge of scavenged TNT under one parking place. The village had been left ungarrisoned during the day, and Charlie had struck again.

Digging and probing, we unearthed the charge and its detonator. Commo wires led off across the paddy from the blasting cap and, after dark, we traced them down. They terminated in a clump of bushes where the VC had hidden a charged car battery. We could have shorted the battery or rolled up the wire, but American minds don't work that way. Instead, we dug up the explosives, adding them to our supplies, and parked the Apostle over the hole.

Then we wired a light bulb to Charlie's firing circuit, and swung the gun to cover that bush. That's the only time I've seen GIs competing for guard duty—everybody wanted to be in at the climax. At 0300 the light glowed dimly, and the 90mm went off with a crash that woke the whole camp.

"Dead hit, Sarge," said the squad leader who'd been sent out to investigate.

"Well, is there anything left?"

"Just this," he said, holding up a foot and ankle clad in a rubber sandal.

That was about the only positive result of the entire action. The brass finally made the decision to go back to small-scale operations that covered more territory, and didn't drive off the quarry with massive amounts of men and machinery.

Since the platoon was, for once, all in one place, Company Headquarters sent out a Chinook cargo chopper for a full resupply. The helicopter carried our fuel in huge rubber bags slung beneath its fuselage, and the pilot first dropped them off, then settled in to unload internal cargo. Part of the load was a returning crewman who brought us news of the company's other platoons.

"First is still up on the high road to Pleiku, acting like pillboxes. But 2d is on coast patrol again—and they just lost Lieutenant Nolan!"

"What happened?" we asked in chorus.

"What you might expect," he replied. "A two-bit, one-platoon firefight. He took a rocket in the chest because he was head-and-shoulders out of the turret."

Saddened by the news, we nonetheless finished our refueling, pressurizing the fuel bladders by running one track up on them. Resupply completed, we went our separate ways, assigned to new infantry units.

By this time. I'd been in-country and in combat long enough to be trusted with a tank, as long as there was an experienced TC along to hold my hand in case anything got sticky. (We almost never operated completely alone anyway, because a VC could slip in under your guns and plant a charge in your tracks.) This meant that anytime a TC went on R&R or sick call, I got that tank for a while. As a result, I got one hell of a lot of very valuable experience.

There was a chronic shortage of troops and some tanks operated with three- or even two-man crews. This created a situation where, when one vehicle needed repairs that couldn't be accomplished in the field, that tank, along with the driver and an escort to the road, was given to—that little old general-purpose tanker—me. At one time or another, I must have brought in every crippled machine in the platoon, fixed it up, and brought it back, only to have another damaged one foisted on me. No complaints though; it gave me a lot of time in company base.

No complaints, but one regret—I wasn't there when Pappy got hit. Sergeant Quinton, our First Shirt, had decided to spend a few days with the troops in the field and had taken a hit—par for the course. He never got nailed seriously, but it seemed that whenever he went to the field, the VC jumped whomever he visited. This time was no exception, and I felt like a lost soul as I heard all my buddies going into a hell of a firefight without Holt, Witt, and me. The Ape had taken too much mine damage, and we'd brought her in to install new torsion bars.

Sergeant Bell had rotated out, Watanabe was on his way home, and every tank was running with a three-man crew. Third was dangerously low on professionals. Pappy had taken over 3-6, the Assassin, to use its command radios, and the platoon was working with an infantry company between English and Geronimo, over towards the western hill range. The infantry had found a large, ill-organized mixture of Cong with a Chinese cadre, and the resulting battle had degenerated into a large mess, with squad-size units continuously pleading for armored help.

Unfortunately, there wasn't much available. Since the death of Lieutenant Nolan, the company had only three officers. There were only seventeen tanks in the company to begin with, and they were scattered to the winds and the whole Air Cav area was getting hot with VC activity.

First Platoon, pulled from its garrison duty on Highway 19E, was fighting savagely in the An Lao Valley, two ridgelines to the west of us. The 2d, under Lieutenant Walker, was approximately thirty miles south of Bong Son, working for 3d Brigade out of LZ Uplift. Each platoon of five tanks had been "satellited" to one of the division's three brigades. We were spread so thin that, part of the time, the CO couldn't even find all of his tanks—until they went into combat and radioed in.

When 3d Platoon got dragged into what was essentially

a series of small-unit engagements, the only reinforcements available were the HQ tanks, Executioner and Sergeant Black's Widowmaker. They blasted through the main gate at full throttle and roared cross-country at flank speed—but they couldn't possibly reach the site for three hours. Until then, the platoon was on its own.

All work ceased at company base as we clustered around the communications track, a high-top M113 with a radio mast beside it. We could hear the talk between the tanks and, by switching to the infantry and artillery frequencies, monitor the entire battle.

Captain Williams had long since taken his chopper, and was circling over the action. The combat arena was a widespread village complex made up of small hamlets, each of which housed a few bunkers and a small VC unit. Rocket-artillery choppers and gunships poured munitions into infantry-designated targets, but aerial attack can be too indiscriminate. The object was to "demilitarize" the objective, not to destroy it. The area was about a mile-and-a-half square of houses, mixed with forest and plantings, surrounding one of those white-sand ancestral graveyards.

The tanks were dashing across this minidesert at high speed, answering urgent calls for help. This bunch of Charlies had some extremely good snipers and machine gunners, which made life hazardous for our TCs.

Like old-time gunfighters, they stood crouched in the turrets swinging the long nineties with the override. Their heads would emerge for three seconds or less; then they would "shoot from the hip" and duck back to safety before a sniper could draw a bead on them.

The three of us sat in frustrated agony, listening to the urgent communications as the battle progressed. I could hear the howl of the turret motors and the sound of the nineties in close combat as background to the terse conversations. The A-Go-Go, called to rescue a half platoon that had gotten pinned down, charged in a little too fast. A machine gunner who'd been overlooked raked the turret and injured the gunner who was acting as TC. We heard him call for his own medevac, heard him nail that MG and direct his vehicle out of there. The tank now had only two men in it, but it continued to fight.

Just as the medevac lifted out, Assassin hit a mine, and Sp4 Wilson, now commanding the A-Go-Go from his driver's position, pulled alongside the cripple to shield repairs. Before the men could get the new track blocks in place, a sniper zapped Wilson's last crewman, a Pfc. loader. He was medevacked out, but not before Assassin's gunner had terminated the sniper.

Wilson was now the only man in the tank. Pappy was just ordering him to clear out and find a safe place when a burst of tracer swept across the turret and put a hole in the platoon sergeant's shoulder. By then, the two headquarters tanks had arrived, providing two experienced tank commanders. Pappy was airlifted out and Black took temporary command of the platoon. We'd lost three good men in half an hour.

An infantry squad leader called in asking for a tank to silence an emplacement that his men couldn't approach. To our surprise, Wilson answered, "Roger that, this is Chopper 3-5, where are you?" The squad leader said he was due north of "those two tanks in the middle of the tombstones." At this time, Black did not know that Wilson was alone. All Wilson knew was that, if we could help it, 3d Platoon *never* let an infantryman die.

He drove A-Go-Go up to the squad's position, crawled into the turret, loaded the 90mm, checked the co-ax feed, and dropped into the gunner's seat. Leaving the turret hatches shut, he alternately fired the gun, got up, loaded it, and returned to the sights. After neutralizing that menace, he took out an LMG for another squad, using the co-ax. Then someone else called for help. He swung the turret dead rear, opening a passage into the driver's box, and taking those controls, he drove to where he was needed, repeating the amazing performance time after time.

Erwin Rommel once defined a tank as "an iron box containing courage." We listened, awestruck, as for four long hours Wilson did the jobs of four highly skilled men—singlehanded. Awarded the Silver Star for that feat, he later told me, "I just got so damn mad I went cold—all I wanted was blood!"

That battle cost us our last leader and, with Pappy gone and no lieutenant, we needed a transfusion. We got one all right—E7 Hazelip from 2d Platoon. The Ape was at company base, and the platoon was on its way in. Second had almost a full complement of troops, so Captain Williams detached their senior tank commander, Sfc. Hazelip, made him our platoon honcho, and brought him into English to meet the crews.

Known as "Sergeant Death," his nickname was well-earned. He had some strange ways and, at first, we didn't get along. For one thing, never having been a command noncom before, his idea of crew cooperation was that we three were the crew, and we should do all the work. This was his standing order: "I want this tank hot and ready, with my helmet resting on the cupola, anytime I walk up here; and that's your job, Sergeant Zumbro."

"Christ," I thought, "a prima donna!"

In the four months I had already spent in-country, there had been some fairly interesting firefights; and all concerned had handled themselves well. Hazelip, however, never missed a single detail; he seemed to have eyes in the back of his head out in Charlie country and, while he was a hard driver, he had a lot to teach. The trick of "hip-shooting'' the turret, for instance, had been looked down upon as being ineffective for the main gun beyond a few yards. But bringing his skills from An Lao Valley, Hazelip's method used the cupola-mounted .50 as a ''donkey sight,'' adjusting it to be parallel with the 90mm. That took care of traverse; by looking over the muzzle of the .50, a TC could be sure of hits with the cannon. By putting his foot on the breech shield, he could feel elevation and know what the gun was doing. The 7.62mm coaxial machine gun had the same trajectory as the 90mm H.E.P., so he used the co-ax as a ''spotter.''

When we went back out on patrol, working north and west of LZ English, these and other tricks had spread through the platoon, and our effectiveness had increased radically. By having the gunners at the sights continuously, searching the brush through the 10-power telescopes, we spotted many potential ambushes long before the infantry walked into them. With five tanks to a platoon, each one took a segment of the horizon and scanned closely, using the sights to peer into shadows where normal vision wouldn't penetrate. One incident serves to illustrate just how effective the procedure was.

''Sarge, I got a slope in the bushes; he's laying low and staring dead at us.''

''Well, put a burst over his head,'' Hazelip said.

The Cong took off like a bat out of hell; he was armed, so I shifted the sights and kept the triggers down. This increased pressure on the VC, predictably, incited fights where normally they would have let us go by. Well, that was what we were there for.

The Ape was busting bunkers for an infantry platoon in a little hamlet about twenty miles north of Bong Son, when an acute sniper problem developed. This hamlet, one of a group that made up a sizable village, turned out to be fortified, and we were having a tough go at it. We'd lost five riflemen to the same damn sniper. Hazelip drove him back into cover with the 90mm, but he seemed to be bulletproof.

"The hell with this fooling around," he said. "Holt, drive us in there and neutral steer—we'll grind his ass out." But to our surprise, the tracks only lifted slightly and didn't dig in.

"I got an idea, Sarge."

"Okay Zippo, let's hear it."

"We can pop him out like a zit. If we can get one track up on that bunker next to the hootch, I can get enough depression to put a delay shell *under* him." A couple of minutes later we were in position; and—Wham!

The sniper was in a spider hole (roofed-over foxhole) inside a half-destroyed shack, and previous shells had simply bounced off his ground-level roof. The delay shell, set to explode .05 seconds after contact, went off directly beneath him. The combination of shell and muzzle blast completely engulfed the tank with smoke, dust, and falling debris. We were blinded and halfway asphyxiated, but we crawled out of the hatches just in time to hear an infantryman yell, "Hey, look at supergook!" The pressure wave of the detonation had launched the sniper like a human cannonball in a steep parabola, and his body disappeared over a distant roof.

This caused some measure of hilarity, all too rare in combat. When the Assassin's new driver screwed up as he took out a house, the firefight started to turn into a circus.

The right technique in taking out a house is never to hit the center of the building, because the roof will fall on the turret as the walls collapse. Usually we would peel off one wall and shoot back into the opening, but the new man drove right through the center. The result was a detached roof running through the battle with tracks under it, and curses coming out of it.

As if this wasn't bad enough, the infantry had started to round up prisoners, and one squad leader had gotten the bright idea of securing his group to the Apostle. Using commo wire, he had tied them in a row, each man's hands tied to the neck of the one in front. He had then taken the lead prisoner's hands and fastened them to the tank's trailer hitch, slamming the tow ring shut on the wire. However, he neglected to inform the TC; the vehicle passed in front of us, cruising at an easy fifteen miles per hour—with a string of captives high-stepping desperately behind him.

"Slow down 3-2, before you kill 'em."

"Kill who? The fight's over."

"Look behind you. You've got a tail."

"Well, don't blame me. I didn't put them there." Just then, one very bothered squad leader showed up to claim his prizes—and we all had a good laugh.

We weren't the only ones having green-troop problems. Later that night, one of the squad leaders got lost on patrol. The infantry captain came over to us and said, "I've got a lost sheep out there who's going to be a supply sergeant when, and if, I get him back. Can you help me locate him?"

"Could be," Hazelip said. "Which direction did he head off in?"

"Due south, and he can't be too far, I've still got him on the radio. But he's lost his sense of direction and seems to have panicked."

Having a rough idea of what was coming next, I had the engine ticking over. "Zumbro," Hazelip said, "ease out into the open and see if you can pick them up on infrared." Holt eased us out in the open and, after switching on the searchlight, I dropped in the gunner's seat to begin scanning. Hazelip walked to the rear of the hull and picked up the external handset, so he could talk to us as well as to the captain.

"I got 'em, Sarge," I said, "about 195 degrees, and dang near out of IR range." The CO should have been able to direct his "sheep" in with that information, but that fella was actually lost in the open.

"The hell with this fooling around," the captain said, taking the handset. "You in there, put that thing on white light."

I reached up and twisted the control over.

Immediately a startled voice came in on the infantry frequency, "What the fuck is that!"

"Never mind, goddammit, just follow it home, and report to me when you get here."

Not for anything would I have been in that man's shoes. Working for hard-driving Hazelip was bad enough, but at least we were all competent and that kept some of the heat off. The trouble was, our new boss couldn't shut himself down after combat; he was always in overdrive. One gunner's comment summed it up for all of us: "Too bad we can't figure some way to freeze him solid and carry him around in a cooler. That way, all we'd have to do would be thaw him out and set him in the turret when we're in action."

The next day we got the word to return to English for a maintenance break. All we had to do was check out a couple of villages on the way.

Chapter Five

DEATH AND RESURRECTION OF THE APOSTLE

The kids didn't show up for handouts or to sell produce, and the village had all the hallmarks of an ambush. We were walking lightly, with safeties off. In such circumstances, rather than penetrate the villages, we would stick to the open spaces between them—the green fields, the dry paddies, sometimes the white-sand graveyards.

With gun tubes moving nervously, like hunting dogs casting for a scent, we were in a graveyard, with the Apostle leading and the rest of the tanks strung out in a rough echelon formation, turrets searching for hostiles. Our command tank, the Ape, was in the center of the formation. As the situation didn't look too bad yet, I switched places with Witt, putting him in the gunner's seat, while I stood with my head out of the loader's hatch searching the trees with binoculars. The nearest infantry was miles out of reach, and we were on our own.

"Three-two, don't enter that treeline. I got a bad feel—" Ka-boom! A towering blast of fire, dust, and smoke issued from the Apostle's left side. The tank commander and the loader flew from the turret in ballistic arcs, launched by the concussion of a huge, jolting explosion. We even felt the shock wave over on our side of the cemetery a hundred yards away. The turret crew of the Apostle landed in the sand some distance from the tank. Since we were carrying an observer, a New Zealand corporal who was tank trained, I stuffed him into the turret and took off. I made a long, flying dive, landing with a paratrooper's roll, and came up in a dead run heading for the smoke and dust that obscured the tank.

Another series of concussions assaulted my ears and I hit the ground, wondering if this was *it*. With relief, I realized the noise was 3d Platoon reacting like a family with a hurt brother. Nineties spitting in all directions, they were rushing to form an iron circle around the one in trouble. I checked out the TC, and found him breathing and not bleeding. I was looking for the loader, when Bronco Kindred, the driver, came staggering around the right track with blood coming from his mouth. Seeing me, he relaxed and fell to the ground, his eyes glazing. I picked up his hand and, feeling a pulse, cradled his head in my left arm.

"What happened, Zippo?" he asked.

"You hit the biggest mine ever laid, and parts of the tracks went in orbit."

"Man, when I fuck up, I do it right," he said, and then passed out.

All of a sudden, the smashed tank's ninety went off in an anticlimactic roar, and a minute later the gunner crawled out, eyes larger than tennis balls. "Man, you never saw anything as black as the inside of that mother." And he, too, passed out on the ground.

Unbelievably, no one was killed, and we weren't taking any fire. The TC had internal concussions, and the loader had a piece of metal in his groin. Bronco's head had been directly under the gun and he'd bounced between the tube and his hatch, causing him no damage other than a bitten tongue and a few loose teeth. Even the gunner, who'd been trapped in the turret, had received only a mild pressure shock. The Apostle, however, would never preach again. The old girl was a wreck.

The hull was lying bow down, heaved over on its left side, in a twenty-foot crater. The entire bottom section of the track and suspension was gone, sheared off at the bolt holes. Even the return rollers, above the curve of the hull, were gone, and what remained of the track was laid out behind the machine like a peeled snake skin. The fenders and sponson boxes also were gone, and the turret was jammed by a twisted fender strut.

Inspecting the inside, we were amazed that there was so little damage. The running gear was wrecked, but the fighting part of it was virtually intact and we each started to covet what we saw as spare parts. But that could wait for later. What counted now was getting our friends out and into good hands.

Already the air was filling with choppers. First the "skin ship," an unarmed medevac Huey, came in and removed the wounded. "Throw their personal bags in with them," Hazelip said. "They won't be coming back to *this* tank." As the medevac lifted out, a pair of gunships howled overhead, taking up stations above Assassin and Avenger who were prowling through the houses, probing with their MGs, trying to roust out the perpetrators. Then a company of infantry landed and fanned out through the area. It soon became apparent that the settlement was nearly abandoned—only a few terrified mama-sans could be found—

and the mine had probably been resting there for a year or more.

Our CO, Captain Williams, arrived on the scene to check over the damage and decide what to do with the wreckage. "Well, we certainly aren't going to leave it here for Charlie to scavenge, and it would take weeks to strip it bare, so we'll have to drag it out."

"Right, sir," Hazelip said. "It will take us three, maybe four days to find and scrounge enough parts and reassemble the left track."

"Do you need a tank retriever?"

"No sir, but we may need more parts than we have or can police up, and we'll definitely need more bolts than we carry." The captain went back with a requisition list and the rest of us set about cannibalizing a set of tracks for our cripple. A platoon of ground-pounders stayed for security, so we all could work on the wreckage.

I question if tank crews in any other army on earth could pull off what we did in those three days. First, we went on a monumental police call, digging parts out of houses, streams, and trees, where they had landed after the blast. Most of the running gear was too heavy to be man-portable, so whoever found a section had to wait for a work detail and a tank to come and get it.

Next, using a combination of self-rescue techniques, we pulled the tank upright, jacked it high enough to relieve the torsion bars, and started bolting suspension arms and road wheels (we found one set a full quarter-mile away) back on. By the end of the third day after the catastrophe, we were moving—headed for the highway.

Back at company base, the work wasn't over by a long shot. We had to pull all the usable parts for "controlled cannibalization." This is supposed to be a very orderly process but, in practice, the pitter-patter of feet in the dark never ceased. At any rate, the job was done and the sorely needed spares got where they would do the most good.

The temporary leftovers were stored in the "parts facility." This was a one-ton trailer full of miscellaneous armored-company pieces. Whoever wanted a part, just dug into the trailer, throwing junk out onto a tarp, until he found his prize. The next customer reversed the process, throwing parts back up into the trailer, thus maintaining an orderly balance.

By rare good fortune, one of our other platoons, the 2d, was in base at the same time, so we had the chance to renew old friendships—and to take advantage of Patterson, their torsion-bar specialist. No one ever designed armored equipment for the kind of misuse that ours were receiving, so the heavy steel bars of the suspension needed constant replacing. Unfortunately, since the "experts" who designed the machines had made no provisions for repairs, it was necessary to cut through the armor with an acetylene torch, then beat the stub of a broken bar out with a twenty-pound sledge and a wrecking beam.

Normally, the job took an hour or two of hammering, sweating, and cussing—along with the usual scraped elbows and skinned knuckles. But with Pat around, the process went more like this:

"Hold that bar a little lower, Zippo."

"Right, are you gonna hit now?"

"No. Forward a hair, and a little more down."

"Christ, just how lon—?"

Whang! And the stub shot out clean, leaving you ready to begin reassembly. It was fast and simple, and he charged only a six-pack per bar, deliverable after 1800 hours.

Being temporarily back at base didn't stop company action. The radios still bounced one section or another out at odd hours, and we found out that 2d Platoon was as wild as we were.

One night the infantry down south of Bong Son called for help, only to be told that everything that could move was out and working. The ground CO was still pleading that he desperately needed searchlight and direct fire, so a couple of 2d Platoon crazies volunteered their broken-down tanks. One had a dead turret. The other could shoot, but had lost its transmission seals and couldn't run. They coupled the two together with tow cables and the "runner" pulled the "shooter" into position and got the job done, after a fashion.

Our 3d Platoon was just about refitted when Hazelip did a friend a favor that led to a direct confrontation between us. Second Platoon was on a short mission, and one of its command vehicles was undergoing repairs, so Hazelip offered to lend the Ape to his buddy. This didn't set well with us but, what the hell, we were there to do a job.

But when the tank was returned, it was a mess. Crud on the turret floor was inches deep; all of the sponson boxes were open, and full of leaves and mud. The worst part of it, though, was that half of the tools and gear that are used for normal maintenance seemed to be missing.

"Zumbro, goddamn you, where is all the gear?"

"Sergeant Hazelip, when you ordered me to turn the tank over to 2d, every damn piece of gear was on it—and it was clean."

"I don't believe you. My friend wouldn't misuse my tank. Now get in there and clean your mess up."

Seething, I worked fast, knowing I didn't have much time. The gear *had* to be there in the mud, I reasoned, or they couldn't have run the tank for that long. Sure enough, it was all there, but buried in dirt and leaves. After sorting and stacking it on the back deck, I went looking for the sergeant, certain that what I had found would make him see reason. I had misjudged his rage.

"Goddamn you, Zumbro, I didn't give you permission

to leave that tank. Now get up on 3-2 with those privates where you belong, and work on it for a while."

Gritting my teeth and girding my patience, I obeyed, because now half the company was watching.

"Why do you let him do that?" one of the base-camp Pfcs asked. "You could have him up before Top for half of what he's said."

"Because I don't want this to get that far."

By now, "The Lip" was coming back, fairly frothing at the mouth. "That tank is still as cruddy as ever! What the—?"

"Sergeant Hazelip!" I roared. "Every piece of gear you accused me of losing is on the back deck! I dug it out of the mud."

This seemed to make him even madder, if that were possible, and, reaching up to where I stood on the fender, he grabbed my leg. Then his eyes widened; he stopped, let go, and stalked back to 3-4. Whether he caught himself or noticed my hands, I don't know. But that sudden calming saved us from a very nasty incident, for I had forgotten that I was armed, and my right hand had, of its own volition, moved ever so slightly. Afterwards, I rounded up Holt and Wittlinger and we tore into the mess that was our home. The sergeant was gone for a *long* time.

"Zumbro, we've got to talk," Hazelip said, intercepting me on the way to supper. I stood there waiting for him to break the silence. "You're a good sergeant," he said. "There's no reason for a feud."

"How about cutting me and the crew a little slack. You want the tank to be maintained by us, and ready to go when you walk up to it, right?"

"Well, yes."

"Then let us do it our way. It works for us. And don't come bellowing up and telling us to do it your way or else. Sarge, can't you ever turn it off? You're the best combat commander I've ever seen, but it's like you're stuck in overdrive, and we have to take as much from you as the VC does.''

After more of this back-and-forth, we finally came to an accommodation. I won't go so far as to say we ever became friends, but we worked well together and that helped the outfit, which was the most important thing. No machine works well when there is friction in the gears, and friction in a combat machine can get its members killed.

The next day, we got the good news. The Apostle's crew had recovered from their injuries; they had already been issued their new tank, and were on their way up the coast on a landing craft (LCM). The grapevine passed the information to the crews before command heard it, so engines were ticking over before Sergeant Quinton called for Hazelip. The run over to the coast was through a fairly secure zone, and we treated it as an outing, rather than as a mission.

Not long after we had settled on the beach, we could see the LCM approaching—which brought back to the older members memories of the company's original voyage. ''Zippo,'' one of the gunners asked, ''did anyone ever tell you how nervous the LCVP skipper was?''

''Well no,'' I said, bracing myself for a tale.

''That was one nervous buck. Seems there'd been a couple of North Vietnamese torpedo boats in the area and he was unarmed, except for two .50s. He kept pacing the bridge and peering into the radar room, expecting to see blips any minute.

''Captain Williams told him, 'Look, you're not unarmed at all. There's a company of tanks in the hold. Tell you what. If you see trouble, just point your bow at them, open the landing doors, and my boys will take care of it.' "

After the laughter died down, a semiserious discussion got started. We were trying to decide if it really would have worked. Then we saw the new Apostle up close, and we all waited as the ramp was let down into the gentle surf just offshore. With a wave and a cheer they came charging down.

And they kept coming down—farther and farther, past the driver's hatch, past the fenders, and even farther as blue salt water covered the muzzle of the ninety. The tracks went frantically into reverse, slipping uselessly on the steel ramp, as the momentum carried the brand-new tank to a watery doom. On it came. Now the turret was under water and the driver popped up like a cork and was swimming for shore. Now the turret crew were hip-deep in seawater, standing disconsolately on their submerged steed, their faces expressing the resigned horror of Wile E. Coyote going over a cliff.

We stared in utter disbelief as, one by one, they swam ashore. By pure bad luck, the LCM had beached on a hidden offshore bar that had a tide-dredged hole behind it. The skipper had picked the only scour-hole for a hundred yards, so the tank went in up to the antennas.

We waded in, hooked up the tow cables, dragged the wreck out, and began trying to salvage something. Bronco crawled into the driver's box, reached down, and pulled the emergency escape lever. A cascade of seawater poured out as the belly hatch dropped open. After the crew retrieved their gear and spread it out to dry, we set about trying to undo the damage.

Privately I had my doubts, having worked as a salvage diver between enlistments, but we had to try. For two solid hours, we towed the useless hulk up and down the beach, attempting to "jerk-start" the diesel—all to no avail. Salt water had gotten into the whole electrical system, and apparently also into the engine cylinders, blocking the pistons.

No blame could be applied and no charges were filed, but that was one depressed bunch of GIs who towed another deceased tank back to company base. Several weeks later, another one was delivered, and this time the LCM coxswain was very picky about his landing point.

In the meantime, our pattern of operations was changing. We were operating more out of company base, instead of remote LZs, and life was a lot easier for a while. We got more time in "town," and more time off, after we caught up on maintenance and repairs. Most of our call-outs were one- or two-day scoot-and-shoot missions, and the war seemed to be slowing down temporarily. These periods never lasted long for A Company, so we set out to enjoy ourselves as much as possible.

Chapter Six

BONG SON CITY

Going on pass in Vietnam wasn't exactly the same as in Germany or the States where, when a GI is turned loose on unsuspecting civilians, his officers do all that is possible to make sure he is "safe." That means no brass 'nucks, switchblades, chains, needle knives, or other social equalizers. The situation in Bong Son required that those rules be reversed, and the MP at the gate was ordered to see that each departing soldier was armed and dangerous.

Bong Son City was large, compared to the towns we were used to. The streets, though paved, did boast a few cement-block buildings, some even two stories tall—and one towering edifice of three stories. We all agreed that nothing there would stop a tank, should the need ever arise. (Unless one of the larger buildings had a basement. Holes in the ground are anathema to heavy combat machines, and falling into basements is a source of nightmares.)

After an extended haircut, we wandered through the downtown "loop," soaking up atmosphere and looking for something to blow excess piasters on. There were many shops and stores—more than in the rural market towns. The war didn't seem to have interrupted normal trade; we found luxury goods such as star sapphires from Thailand, as well as utility items. Open-air stalls and peddlers' carts lined the streets, but behind them the permanent businesses of the town were in electrically lighted buildings.

We found a sidewalk restaurant that suited us and tried, with the help of a friendly National Policeman, to sort out the menu. (Rule two in Vietnamese cuisine: if the menu says monkey, do not look in the kitchen—a skinned monkey resembles a dead baby.) We settled for fish, vegetables, and rice—our police friend showed us how to use chopsticks.

With the aid of his English and our butchered Vietnamese, we learned quite a lot about the local culture; at the same time, he satisfied his curiosity about America. (I hope to hell he got out in '75.) Finally, it took only one question to break the conversation. Stanley, from our headquarters section, asked him why a jeweler would be drilling holes in watch crystals. We'd seen this earlier in a small jewelry stall in the market and hadn't been able to figure out why someone would ruin a perfectly good watch lens.

Our policeman's eyes narrowed and he growled one word: "Where?"

Anticipating a little excitement, we told him, and he asked us to go back to the place, casually, while he rounded up a few of his men. Sure enough, while the old proprietor was showing us some "Swiss" watches, a younger man still sat in the rear operating a crude, string-powered pump drill, putting tiny holes in crystals that looked to be pocketwatch size. Without warning, our policeman came through the back, and armed men appeared on each side of us. We drew our .45s, watching nervously until we recognized them as the policemen who had been patrolling the streets.

As the fuzz dragged the jewelers away, our friend explained: "Hole in watch makes what Americans call booby trap. One wire here, to battery and explosive; other to watch, and back to battery."

Very tricky! When the hand came around and touched the wire that would be cemented in the hole, a blasting cap made of a taillight bulb would set off the explosive. He followed this explanation with a short familiarization lecture on bicycle bombs, and we assured him that we would steer clear of bikes with battery-powered headlights, from then on.

This incident created in us a desire for a cool, alcoholic drink, so we headed for the company's favorite cathouse, intending to get slightly loose and swap yarns with whatever crews might be in town. Several troopers were on the porch, drinking Korean "45" beer and watching the life of the city. Inside, in the tapestry-hung "clubroom," the dozer crew had commandeered a table next to the bar, and were making business arrangements with the girls.

Their gunner, Roman Sanchez, was of Mexican extraction, was Catholic, and married, so he didn't experiment with the native stuff. When the rest of the crew went upstairs, he wandered over.

"Hey, Sanchez," Stanley said, "you look naked. Where's your hardware?"

To answer, he opened his jungle shirt, revealing a shoulder-holstered Colt and a half-dozen M26 frags. Setting his beer on the lacquered table, he pulled up a chair, reversed it and, resting his arms on the back, announced: "We're all dead again."

"Can't be," I said. "This ain't quite bad enough to be hell, but it sure ain't heaven. And I ain't Catholic, so that leaves out purgatory."

"We have to be," he continued. "I got it straight from 'Hanoi Hannah.' This is the third time since the 69th hit this country that we've been wiped out to the last man and tank by defenders of the revolution." Radio Hanoi was a source of much amusement during a GI's tour, because it was about as far off base as you could get and still be talking about the same war.

We all had a good laugh and expressed our opinions of the Cong and the NVA. Then our laughter was cut short by the unmistakable vibration of heavy armor. A tank was on the move, so we all went out to see, checking our weapons as we walked onto the porch.

"Christ," George, our New Zealand observer, said, speaking for all of us, "we should have stayed in camp. Will you look at what that bloody Assassin has pulled off."

There was the 3-6, freshly washed, coming down the main drag with Red Cross girls—real, honest-to-God, Caucasian women—perched on each side of the turret. They were drawing the stares of Vietnamese and GIs alike, and the crew all had Cheshire-cat grins on their faces. Periodically, some high-ranking brass of the Air Force or Air Cavalry would take a notion to "inspect" the armored contingent, so we all took turns with what our exec, Lieutenant Walker, called PR work: giving demonstration rides and familiarization lectures. *This*, however, was something new, and we'd all been upstaged.

At intervals, the Red Cross and the USO entertainers came around on morale visits. Ordinarily they distributed top-ten records for which we had no players, and romance novels, or westerns which, in comparison to our real lives, were terribly dull. One of them even thought we needed puzzles to exercise our imaginations, and brought us some of those little wire-and-bent-nail deals.

"Try this one, soldier," she said. "No one's ever managed to take the two nails apart."

Bronco, dead-dog-tired from almost single-handedly rebuilding a suspension system, took the puzzle, hauled out a pair of wire cutters, and snipped the nails neatly in two.

"You never gave it to a tanker, Miss," he said very respectfully, trying to keep a straight face.

We did need something to laugh about now and then. Somehow the folks back home never understood what was really going on in Southeast Asia; their attempts to provide entertainment could produce tragicomic results.

Take the movies that were shipped over, for instance. Can you imagine anything less interesting to a combat soldier than reruns of the TV series "Combat"? Instead of Marilyn Monroe or Jane Russell in living color, we got Vic Morrow and Rick Jason in black-and-white. Not only was the fare old hat, compared to the war, but the location was hazardous to our health. The movie screen was outdoors, within easy rifle shot of the perimeter wire; this fact did not go unnoticed by the VC.

One night the show, such as it was, received a startling interruption. During one of the noisier combat scenes, one of the GIs down in the front row began screaming bloody murder.

His buddy stood up and shouted, "Live fire! The gooks are shooting through the screen!" He hit the dirt with, "Turn that goddamn thing off!"

The projectionist cut the lights, but shots kept coming until we were all out of there. A tank up on the ridgeline picked up the source of aggravation, and stitched the area with co-ax, driving the snipers away.

* * *

The only difference between a command tank and a regular tank is a set of trick radios that allow the tank commander to monitor extra frequencies. Each platoon had two command tanks: one for the platoon leader—the "6"; and one for the command sergeant—the "4." Since we had no officer, the Assassin, 3-6, was running around loose, acting as a line combatant. Hazelip was commanding the unit from Ape's turret.

The morning after the movie sniper incident, we saw Hazelip coming in with a new man. Holt was speculating about who would get the "fresh meat," when the more observant Wittlinger said, "Look who's carrying the new man's gear, Sarge." Well glory be, Hazelip handed the replacement's gear to a Headquarters Pfc., and pointed toward the Avenger. At last, we had an officer.

Lt. Joe Somolik was just what the doctor ordered. Some who spout military theory would have us believe there is such a thing as a universal leader who can be stamped out of schools like OCS and the NCO academies; but in real life the personalities must be compatible or the unit will suffer and, in our position, that could be fatal. After adjusting and acclimatizing, Lieutenant Joe fit the 3d like a long-lost prodigal.

We were on orders for a spell of convoy duty, and that was a perfect way to conduct orientation for the new man.

"Sergeant Zumbro," Lieutenant Somolik said, "my gunner has gone on R&R so, until he returns, Sergeant Hazelip has agreed to lend you to me. You're to keep me from doing anything stupid."

Having paralyzed my vocal cords with that announcement, he went on.

"Look Sarge, I'm a westside-Chicago Cicero kid who went into the Army to stay out of trouble. I went through OCS and I've had the usual armor training, but I have no practical experience. The platoon sergeant says you're one of the best [ya coulda fooled me], so let's take this thing out and play with it.''

On reflection, I figured out why I was picked for that particular job. Several weeks before, the platoon had been in a little scuffle with some neighborhood VC with delusions of grandeur. Watanabe had rotated out and, with his replacement not in yet, I'd been sent out to command the A-Go-Go with our New Zealand major as loader; I thus had experience in tactfully instructing officers.

This officer, Lieutenant Joe, was not normal by any standards. He insisted on a crash course in crew duties, as well as a Vietnam indoctrination. So for a week, the Assassin hardly stopped as he put himself through all of the crew positions, learning the tasks of loader, gunner, and driver, as well as of tank boss. He spent his evenings either with the crews, listening to them recount savage battles, or with the officers in the command bunker, learning the tricks of getting helicopter supplies delivered on time, and how to deal with infantry commanders. This was definitely not the typical new lieutenant—not at all. But then, we had to have someone special, because 3d was special. He'd already figured that out himself, but if he had any doubt remaining, the call-out to the Bong Son river crossing should have erased them.

An infantry company was jumped at a ford, upriver and west of the city, and they called for a little direct-fire gunnery.

Somolik had 3d Platoon winding up, but only a Sp5 gunner was around for A-Go-Go. Its other two men were on leave in town.

''Just give me a head start,'' the gunner pleaded. ''I know where those two are, and you'll have to go through town to make the turn onto the river road, anyway.''

The lieutenant glanced at Hazelip, who nodded, giving

his okay. A mechanic who knew how to drive a tank was in the hatch warming up the diesel, and the two of them drove off. (If they had known about it, I seriously doubt the captain or exec would have approved of that maneuver.)

When we arrived in town, we found the A-Go-Go parked alongside a whorehouse, the fenders scraping a wall, and the Sp5 yelling into a second-story window. As we went by, the missing tankers came out the window, wearing only boots, shirts, and gunbelts and, holding their pants in their hands, they jumped to the turret top, disappearing into the hatches. The A-Go-Go backed away from the building, leaving a naked woman calling from the window, "Come back tomorrow; you got plenty credit."

The 3-5 latched onto the tail of the platoon as we made the turn onto the river road and roared out of town. The lieutenant was out in the lead on his first combat mission, looking in all directions at once, trying to spot the enemy and take in the scenery at the same time.

The road was rapidly getting smaller, more overgrown, as we penetrated farther into the brush. The veterans were keeping a wary eye out for vines and branches as we ripped through the countryside. But the lieutenant was not. Suddenly, he was jerked out of his cupola and draped over the back of the turret by an overhanging limb. There was dead silence from everyone, as we clattered along.

Then: "Don't say it, Zippo. I should have been facing forward in heavy cover."

"Welcome to 3d, Lieutenant," we chorused. Over the private intercom, the Ape's crew agreed that we might just have a "keeper."

By the time we arrived at the crossing, the situation was well in hand. There were fewer hostiles than originally estimated; a pair of M42 Dusters that had been within driving distance had handled the task nicely.

On reporting this to Company Headquarters we got new orders: "Run south to LZ Uplift. Put two vehicles on convoy escort and put the heavy section at the disposal of the infantry commander."

We were back in the war.

Chapter Seven

AMBUSH

Uplift was the nominal base of our 2d Platoon, now commanded by Lieutenant Walker who had replaced Lieutenant Nolan after he'd been killed in action. They'd received orders to rendezvous with a battalion of the 5th Infantry and reinforce a sweep south and east of the LZ. Third Platoon's area, north of Bong Son, had cooled down somewhat, so Captain Williams shifted us south to Uplift, trying to keep all bases covered.

As we rolled into the temporary tank park, Lieutenant Walker greeted Joe Somolik with, "Hey, we just had Ben Hur down here!" This brought a flurry of questions, so the lieutenant explained: "You know that some Hollywood movie stars come around for morale visits? Well, yesterday General Tolson flew in with Charlton Heston; and he went nuts over the tanks. He was only supposed to stay about twenty minutes," Walker continued, "but he wanted to hear what we were doing, and even learn how to drive a tank.''

Fascinated by the ''iron chariots,'' Heston had stayed nearly two hours listening to war stories and driving the command tank all over the LZ. He also had accomplished his purpose—raising the platoon's morale sky high!

Landing Zone Uplift was dry, dusty, and barren; its only saving grace was the food. We were assigned rations at a combined mess hall where the head cook really took pride in his work. Third Platoon's arrival coincided with Thanksgiving, and he managed to produce turkey, mince-meat pie, and all the trimmings.

Even on holidays, work went on; Lieutenant Walker took 2d out to the southeast, and we settled back into routine. Our escort duty consisted of picking up segments of truck convoys, known as ''serials,'' and riding herd on them until they were safely at their intended destination. A pair of tanks would be waiting at the south bridge (the closest one to Qui Nhon that would take the weight of an M48) and, as the first vehicle came over it, one tank would lead out setting the pace. After the last truck had passed, the second tank, the ''dust eater,'' would tag along as far back as possible.

We rotated this duty, keeping to a minimum the strain on men and machines. Meanwhile, the heavy section was out in the paddies implementing a brainstorm of the high command. The monsoon season was approaching, and that meant rice-growing time. In order to deny food to the Cong, some genius dreamed up the idea of destroying the paddy dikes and trucking rice in from another area. At our level, that meant babysitting a couple of engineer bulldozers while they scraped the paddies level.

The plan seemed to be working fairly well, and there was very little hostile activity, except for the usual scattered snipings. Even that died off, as we applied pressure on the culprits. The task of paddywrecking went slowly and kept us moving gradually northward as the dozers moved from one field to the next. Meanwhile, we developed a following of children and Coca-Cola girls.

One girl in particular made it a point to be where the section could see her every day, and she always managed to have enough ice for all three crews. Of course, the fact that there was a bit of European blood showing in her face, and more than Asian curves under her Ao-dai, didn't hurt her popularity at all. More than one crew diverted its route just to kid around with the petite beauty.

The dike-smashing was an addition to our normal duties; the searches and sweeps went on but with one new feature—a dog. This was our first experience working with the K-9 Corps, and it was an instant hit. The dog was a coal-black Belgian Shepherd, donated by a rich, elderly lady. His Sp5 handler was very proud of him.

According to the Sp5, the dog's papers read: "Black Prince of Nassau Kennels,"—but we called him Prince. He was trained to find VC, mines, caves, dope; you name it and that furry radar would nail it for you. He even had his own security guard because the VC had started sniping at the dog and his handler.

Sometimes the scene was almost comical. Imagine three tanks and a platoon of infantry stalking slowly through the heat of a tropical afternoon, all dependent on one moist black nose, all fervently hoping there wasn't a lady dog upwind of him. Prince, you see, had been around soldiers too long; the first thing he would do, on entering a new village, would be to plant his noble genes firmly in the local canine population. There must be some strange-looking dogs on the Bong Son Plain by now, unless they all went into the stew pot. (Dog meat is a delicacy in most Asian cultures—and therein hangs a tail.)

We were leveling the earthworks around one well-irrigated area and, in the process, razing old bunkers and filling in combat trenches around deserted habitations, when one farmer decided that Prince was fair game. The Vietnamese method of killing a dog for meat is to pull its tail sharply backward, straightening the animal's spine, and deliver the death blow to the base of its skull with the edge of a board.

When off duty, Prince was a furry mooch, always on the lookout for C rats, fish, or whatever. The farmer decided to take advantage of this apparent good nature to give his family a royal feast. Sneaking up carefully on the unsuspecting shepherd, he reached for the long, tempting tail—board in hand. A crewman started to warn the handler, but he was waved to silence.

"Watch," the man whispered.

Just as the hand touched his fur, Prince spun and presented his impressive heavy armament, accompanied by a thunderous growl. If the farmer hadn't been fast, he would have been nailed on the spot. He was a tank-length away and accelerating, before his board hit the ground, and he actually kept ahead of the dog until they both were out of sight.

"This happens about once a month," the handler explained. We were still chuckling over the show when the dog came trotting back.

On another mission, the dog started circling around a cleared area in an abandoned hamlet, sniffing and pawing the ground. One of the engineers brought over a mine detector and, since it was a model that goes silent over a cavity, he was able to trace out a large cave. Then one of the dozers opened the top, almost falling into the hole in the process. Since the dog did not go on alert, Bronco went down, looked around, and reported finding a huge stash of assorted explosives and ammunition.

The cave was a "blind" stash, a sealed and hidden cache

of supplies, rather than part of a defensive tunnel network, and we decided to deprive the Cong of their reserves of goodies. I was down there in short order. After surveying the stash, I set several charges, rather than haul the aged, sensitive explosives to a single location in the cave. This meant using some of the demolition gear that the platoon carried, some from the engineers, and some fairly new plastique that was in the underground magazine. Flash-light clipped to my belt, backing slowly toward the patch of sky that marked the entrance, I was paying out a roll of detonating cord, and sweating out the last minutes of what had been an unpleasant hour. I regretted even having mentioned my explosives training.

The entire web of explosives was double fused for pos-itive ignition and the fuse cord was timed for a sixty-sec-ond delay. All that remained was to crimp the final pair of caps, light both orange cords and walk, not run, to a safe place; the Ape would be just right. After pulling both igniters, the party adjourned rapidly to the tanks. At one minute, the ground erupted, slowly at first, and then, with unbelievable speed, a great column of dust, smoke, and fire filled the air. Even through the armor, we could feel the concussion.

One of the few blessings of the oncoming monsoon sea-son with its increasing showers was the consequent filling of the irrigation ponds used to fill the paddies. For us, this was a chance to take baths and to get relief from the heat, since we used them as swimming holes. The normal pro-cedure was to set up a perimeter around a pond, post turret sentries, and take turns getting the crud off. This, by the way, was more than a luxury for tankers—those hulls are very close quarters.

The work this morning had been hot and nasty so, set-ting up a rendezvous with our infantry, we headed for the nearest swimming hole. We had also intended to stop and pick up some more ice, but our little Coca-Cola girl wasn't at her usual station.

"She probably took the day off," one man speculated.

"Naw, she's probably got a boyfriend," another guessed.

There was more of this, as we rolled across the paddies, anticipating a cool swim; then we started taking sniper fire.

"Some clown obviously hasn't received the word," Hazelip said, swinging the turret.

Almost casually, we scanned the treeline of a village complex, trying to spot the faint puff of smoke or the spark of a muzzle blast that would give the sniper away. Assassin spotted him first, and snuffed the Charlie with a short, savage burst of .50 caliber.

"Hey, how did you get that M2 to work?" Somolik wanted to know. (The cupola gun on the M48-A3 is the worst combat mount ever devised.)

"Sacrificed a chicken at that Buddhist shrine," was the flippant reply. "Look out, there's more of 'em."

Peering through the sights, magnified at ten-power, I could see more muzzle flashes, and shadowy figures flitting through the brush. It looked like the end of any dreams for a refreshing dip. That was one almighty-stupid bunch of VC—ruining our plans for an outing. We'd been going right past them, minding our own business, and they could have gone free. Instead, they elected to take on a whole platoon. The light section was in from road duty; all five murder machines were freshly fueled and supplied. Okay, fellas, you want to play for keeps—let's go.

The call went out for the closest company of foot-sloggers, and their choppers were soon on the way. Meanwhile, 3d sat tight and methodically removed every rifleman and machine gunner. With those powerful sights, a gunner is sometimes eyeball-to-eyeball with his adversary, and this was one of those fights. We had closed to within less than a hundred yards, and I could actually see the expression change as my tracers ate into a man's body. At odd intervals, a 90mm would go off, and a machine gun and its crew would be blown clear, turning several somersaults before dropping back to earth.

Somolik decided to use this time before the infantry landed to advantage. He ordered Ape and Apostle on a slow circuit of the group of houses and barns from which the firing was coming. His idea, a good one, was to keep the enemy off balance shifting men to keep track of us, and to probe the defenses for a weak spot that would allow us to penetrate with minimum loss of life.

By the time we got back from our circuit of the perimeter, the choppers had landed our ground troops and we could give them news of the weak spot. There wasn't any. We had drawn heavy small-arms fire during the whole trip. Those engineers, by the way, were a pretty salty bunch. They could have bugged out with no loss of face, but they chose to stay, face the dozers into the battle, get under them with their M14s, and snipe at whatever showed. I also noticed they pulled their beer cooler in with them—good troops.

Once the infantry had divided up and attached rifle squads to individual tanks, that bunch of cocksure Charlies got the royal treatment. The 105mm artillery from Uplift reached out and gave them a good shaking up, including smoke; then, as we moved in through the smoke and dust, the gunships appeared.

Usually we had to work without choppers, because under heavy foliage they simply couldn't see to shoot. But on top of being dumb enough to ambush a tank outfit, these idiots had picked a base whose tree cover was thin enough to allow gunships to operate. It's a comfortable feeling for a tanker to have infantry at his side, and a flying fire platform over his head; it really allows a fellow to concentrate on his work.

"Hey in there," came an unexpected voice, "we're taking rifle fire from that hootch to your left front. Can you take them out?" There is an external telephone handset under the right rear fender, just for the squad leaders, but it's always a surprise when one of them uses it.

By now, with sporadic artillery shelling, gunships firing miniguns and rockets, and the steady wham-thump of the nineties, the din was appalling. (My hearing hasn't been right since.) The tank commander swung the override to put me in the general area, and went back to directing artillery on another section of the battle. At first, all that appeared to me was a sprinkle of muzzle flashes in the man-made gloom; but then I began picking out individuals, and gave each one a dozen 7.62mm zingers.

Five of them had been eliminated when a puff of wind parted the smoke long enough for the afternoon sun to illuminate the scene. There, pinned in a shaft of sunlight, was our little Coca-Cola girl. Just as I was about to warn the crew about the noncombatant, she lifted an ancient, French-army rifle and drew down on an American. The distances were close and the sights were excellent. Biting off what I had been about to say, I gave her a burst.

The whole battle was close range. The tank commanders were constantly heaving grenades into the bushes or down beside the hulls to keep RPG teams at bay. There was a heavy crash alongside us, then screaming that could be heard even through the armor. We glanced up in alarm, and there was Hazelip, turning green.

"Apostle flushed a group out of the bushes," he said, "and they ran into our right track. They're still in there—going over and over."

Gradually the character of the combat changed. Where

there had been stubborn defense, there was now maneuver and flow. The VC, realizing their mistake, were desperately trying to escape or surrender. As they scattered through the woods and fields in ever-smaller groups, the gunships had a field day. Third Platoon pulled out one by one to resupply, take a breather, and then go in again to back up the riflemen on mop-up detail.

Customarily after these messes, we did our own checking around the tanks for unpleasant surprises, sometimes having to use M3 grease guns or even Colts when some diehard came out of the woodwork. Then we checked the hootches for portable, compact souvenirs—most of us had already acquired net hammocks, brush knives, and the like. This time, though, we got a little unexpected "entertainment."

The National Police were flown in, and the prisoners were being interrogated—none too gently. Suddenly, there was a shot, and a policeman who'd been investigating an undamaged bunker dropped, shot through the head. He'd gone in with just a flashlight and the place had been occupied.

The police captain and the American intelligence officer still wanted information, however, so they tied a rope to the neck of a captured VC and sent him in to try to talk sense into the occupants. He crawled in, hands behind his back, the leash on his neck, and began talking. Whatever he then called out to the policeman must have been convincing, because they yanked the rope out expecting him to come with it. Instead, his buddies had cut him free, and the end of the line was now attached to a satchel charge with a lit fuse! When the smoke cleared and we came out of our respective holes, the Ape's ninety spoke twice, ending that particular dialogue.

An aid station was set up in our corner of the battle zone and the wounded, both VC and American, were being brought in. In contrast to VC treatment of captured Americans, we treated their wounded as well as we treated our own—even at some risk because some were known to have hidden grenades. One kid, no older than fifteen, wearing nothing but a loincloth, came walking in under his own power with half his arm missing—no bandage, no tourniquet, nothing; a .50 tracer had cooked the meat, staunching the flow of blood.

Medevac was lifting out the last casualties. I saw an American lying face down on a stretcher, with bandages all over his back, out on morphine.

"What happened to him?" I asked the medic.

"Too many John Wayne movies. He chucked a grenade into a house and flattened himself against the wall the way they do in the movies. But he forgot that these are only bamboo walls, and his own frag nailed him." It didn't seem right to laugh at an injured man, but we had to chuckle a bit.

The humor stopped for me when I saw the girl again. An aged mama-san was crouched under a propped-up section of charred thatch roof, cradling the girl's head in her lap and wailing her heart out. None of the other men saw them, and there was some speculation days later on what had happened to our Eurasian dream girl. Not knowing how many GIs those dark eyes had sighted on, I kept silent and tried to forget that smoke-encircled, sun-dappled clearing.

Chapter Eight

ROAD TO PLEIKU

Monsoon. The word conjures up images of cloud-darkened skies pouring endless deluges on a hapless earth. In our case, the season meant heavy, regular, almost scheduled, afternoon and evening downpours, and intermittent daily showers; wet and soggy, but not an endless downpour. Our mobility was affected more than anything else. While tanks could cross paddies in the wet season, we couldn't maneuver in them; one overly-sharp turn, and we are buried until the VTR (tank retriever) gets there.

We learned early on to "read" the sogginess of a planted section by observing the brightness of the rice sprouts. Light green meant the rice was recently planted and the mud shallow. A darker, richer color meant transplanted crops and deep, soft, track-swallowing goop. A circular clear spot amid the seedlings indicated a bomb crater, and more than one crew was embarrassed by going in one up to the fenders, and having to be hauled out.

For these reasons among others, the decision was made to pull A Company out of the lowlands and put us to work in the highlands, where enemy activity was on the rise. After the hectic battle west of Uplift, the two maneuver platoons were assembled at our base at LZ English, and the task of getting ready to move began.

Not all the tanks were capable of independent travel. At least one would have to be towed by the VTR, and several others required extensive running-gear repairs. By pitching in and organizing special details, such as track-repair crews and electrical teams, headed by specialists from company motor pool who regularly did ordnance-level repairs, we got the job done.

One supply facility in the Air Cavalry, though, was difficult to deal with, and required exceptional treatment. Because they had an IG (Inspector General) inspection coming (in a *combat zone*), they refused to release some of the parts we needed. (That same division had lost its colors in Korea by pulling inspections in a war zone and getting attacked while doing it.) Fortunately, enough hardcore VC were still in the area to generate a few mortar bombardments—and that was all the cover our mechanics needed.

They laid their plans in advance. Then, one rainy night during a sporadic barrage, they loaded into an APC, ran across the runway, and set off a small charge, carefully tailored to simulate a mortar shell, against the corner of the warehouse that held our needed supplies and parts. Using the PC as a base, they raided through the supply stacks, selecting parts and hauling them back to the waiting carrier. By using existing track marks and the rain to mask their tread prints, they made a traceless withdrawal and were back at the tank park before the mortar attack was over. The voltage regulators, hydraulics, and other necessities were distributed long before dawn. This was "midnight requisition" with a vengeance.

In recognition and appreciation of our efforts "above and beyond the call," the Air Cav had certificates of appreciation printed up and planned a ceremony to pass them out to each tanker. Preparation for this caused a small amount of confusion on our part, as such luxuries as clean, greaseless uniforms, fatigue caps, and even shoe polish, were in short supply. Eventually, we got a passable formation together and marched up to Division Headquarters, where the commanding officer, Maj. Gen. John Tolson, personally presented our certificates, along with a mercifully short-winded speech.

Formalities over, the company prepared to move, rolling up the tents, turning over the bunkers to Cav troopers and, in general, cleaning up our mess. We prided ourselves on leaving behind us clean camps and wrecked combat zones; and my last memory of that base is the sight of Hiemes and the dozer tank backblading the entire tank park smooth. Leaving the light vehicles, the PCs and trucks, to find their own way overland, the company's muscle and the VTR headed for the beach where our seaborne transport waited.

Since the landing ship that originally brought the tanks up the coast was no longer available, we now depended on LCMs operated by the Army Transportation Corps— each just large enough for an individual machine. As we came over the last of the coastal hills, eighteen of these were drawn up on the beach, and we were happy to see that the ramps were on solid ground. The baptizing of the Apostle was indelibly imprinted in our minds.

As each tank came out of the woods, Lieutenant Walker, acting as temporary "beachmaster," would direct it to a waiting landing craft, where the LCM crews would ground-guide it into a position on board. Once the last one was securely in place, the flotilla backed away from shore and, in loose formation, ran down the coast to Qui Nhon.

Noting that our gun turret was slightly above the level of the gunwales, I asked the skipper, a Sp6, if tanks had ever been used as river monitors. He told me that it was being considered down in the Delta. We got on well, and after being given a tour of the Ape's interior, he took us through the engine room and accommodations of the LCM. The quarters were a bit crude, but better than we were used to by far.

His engineman and assistant kept the Jimmy diesels spotless, but I was apprehensive about a crack in the hull through which we could see green water streaming past.

"That's nothing serious," he declared. "We beach it at night; and anyhow, the pumps can handle it easily. Ya gotta remember that they're not building new landing craft. This old girl went through half the Pacific landings in World War II, so we've learned to expect some metal fatigue here and there."

I eyed the shore speculatively, measuring the distance with a practiced gunner's vision, hoping that his confidence wasn't the result of misguided optimism.

Beaching without incident outside Qui Nhon City, we pulled up in line, heading up Highway 19E, hearing a sound that belonged in another world. For the first time in what seemed like years, A Company's tracks were clattering on a hard-topped road. Rolling along through the level fields and towns wasn't too strange at first, but then we approached the massive central range of Indochina rising steep and green before us.

The grade looked impossibly steep, but we needn't have worried because the beautifully engineered French highway reduced the mountains to a steady climb, easily negotiable by all types of traffic. As we took the incline, though, a practiced eye could detect the aged, battered condition of the machinery. Here, an engine was ejecting a pure-white vapor, evidence of ill-adjusted or leaking injectors; there, another poured heavy black smoke, indicating clogged air or fuel filters. At every turn, bits of rubber flew from the battered tracks, endangering oncoming civilian traffic. Not one tank had a complete set of fenders, many crews having fabricated temporary track shields from pieces of galvanized culvert, or scrounged sheet metal.

My Lin, our "official" mama-san, chose to follow the tanks on her motor scooter; her sewing machine and all her belongings were being shipped in the supply truck. Her husband, an ARVN tanker, had been killed some years before in a battle during an earlier NVA invasion, and she had attached herself to the American company that destroyed them. Now as she accompanied her "adopted" tanks, the drivers kidded with her and checked the oil and tire pressures in her Vespa.

Every fifty miles, a maintenance halt was called to check the tracks. The individual tread sections, known as "blocs," are held together by heavy links, which in turn are held in place with bolts that tend to come unscrewed as they age. The drivers would stay in the vehicles, moving forward one link at a time, while the rest of us would walk down the length of the hull, tapping the connectors with hammers, searching for the inevitable weak links. Once the maintenance stop was over and all tank commanders reported ready, we were ready for another step toward Pleiku.

Traffic around us was hectic, since the company was noticeably slower than the civilian buses. As oncoming buses, loaded to the roof with people, produce, and livestock, met the impatient drivers who were weaving uphill through our convoy, their rule seemed to be "sound your horn and charge." There were innumerable near misses and several sideswipes, but no serious accidents.

Once we negotiated the first range of green mountains, we were in the central highlands where the character of the land changed. Accustomed to level plains covered with paddies and fields, we now looked out on rolling, jungle-covered hills that appeared as if entire armies could hide in them. In fact, that exactly described the situation, and A Company was to be part of the force that would dig them out.

Our long-lost 1st Platoon was again the guarantor of safe passage along this section of road, dominating the ambush-prone VC with their guns and instant-response capability; and they were as tired and worn as the rest of us. They had each set up a one-tank firebase, and become the center of a small community. Behind the sandbagged fort that each crew had built, a cluster of refugee huts had sprung up, and now, as the company drove by, these were the scenes of farewells. Alerted by radio of the outfit's approach, each 1st Platoon vehicle was ready and waiting and fell into line as we passed—the crew waving a sometimes tearful goodbye to their cluster of Vietnamese adherents. The company was complete again—at least for a few weeks.

We climbed An Khe Pass, the scene of bloody ambushes, and passed the base of the 2d Squadron, 1st Armored Cav. As mile after mile slid by beneath the clattering treads, the land changed even more. Now, along with the Annamese people, who are dominant in Vietnam, we were seeing the fabled Montagnards for the first time. The "hill people" are of medium height, darker, more muscular, and stockier than the lowlanders, and they live, by preference, a thousand years in the past.

As we neared Pleiku and Camp Enari, anticipation began to mount. We had accomplished something that most experts on armored warfare had considered impossible. The tanks had been expected to be no more than rolling pillboxes when they first came to Air Cav, but we proved beyond a doubt that armor could play a decisive role in antiguerrilla warfare. The iron mounts of heavy cavalry had truly "ridden to the sound of the guns," as J.E.B. Stuart once advised; and we had fought as if there were bayonets on the cannons.

We had vowed to return in the same way the company had left, running on our own tracks—not carried in on the backs of tank transporters like broken-down cripples. And, by the gods of war, we had done it. We pulled up outside Pleiku, swept the dust and branches off the hulls, changed to our carefully-bagged, clean uniforms, gave the helmets a quick shot of OD spray paint and, with road guards ahead, drove through the city and into the gates of division base.

We'd known that the rest of the battalion would be waiting, but the last thing anyone expected was the presence of the commanding general, Maj. Gen. W. R. Peers, and the division band. Tradition is not dead. As Company A rounded into the battalion base, the band struck up Custer's old march, the "Garryowen," and played us in. We snapped off an armored salute, swung the tanks into line, and parked. The company had come home in one piece— mission accomplished. Migod, they'd even laid out a cake and a punch bowl. (As we later learned, we were, at that time, the most highly decorated company in the U.S. Army.)

Base camp, oh heavenly day! Hot showers, and fans; cool, smooth, white sheets, and sleep—uninterrupted, blessed sleep. For the first three days, we moved around like automatons, scarcely doing more than eating, sleeping, and anticipating the company party.

The 69th had a private club, and three days after our arrival A took it over for one night and had a blast. We'd already eaten ourselves to the point of satiation, but the cooks prepared snacks and munchies anyway, just in case somebody needed something to soak up the booze.

We couldn't find American entertainers, but Sergeant Quinton managed to scare up a Filipino country-western band that sounded pretty good after a few drinks. It took a few more before the Japanese go-go girls looked acceptable. Once we got roaring, though, a group of GIs took the instruments, sat the band down in the front row, and proceeded to show them how it's done. I don't claim to be an expert on country music, but it sounded fine, and the Filipino lead musician offered to hire them when they got discharged. He told them, "You'll get rich in Manila."

I can still see Dagnall, the dozer tank's driver, listening and saying in disbelief, "Hey, I'm from New York, and I'm beginning to like country music."

As the night wore on, the party got wilder. Some of the American women on base—nurses, USO girls, and others—filtered in. I think they were shocked at the goings-on, because the officers, sergeants, specialists, and privates were all one big, happy, drunk family, and the sky was the limit. The platoon leaders got into a beer-squirting contest, thoroughly drenching themselves and anybody nearby with foaming beer bottles. One lieutenant colonel left after being foamed in the ear.

By this time, the impromptu band had relinquished the instruments to the original combo. Almost anyone can learn to play country music, but the sound of a Filipino vocalist trying to do "The Sons of the Pioneers" was better comedy than the Marx Brothers; some of the guys were laughing so hard they couldn't stand up.

The go-go girls had long since disappeared to wherever girls go at the end of a GI party, when the company finally started to wind down. As a measure of how close we were, that is the only company bash I can remember at which there were no fights—not even cross words. That outfit was truly a "band of brothers."

Partying over, caught up on sleep, we went back to work on the tanks. Down on the coast we'd been barely making do, but now we were experiencing the relative pleasures of a well-stocked armored base camp. Spare parts? No problem. A new turret motor? Just sign here. Transmission problems? "No sweat, Sarge. We'll have a specialist over there in an hour or two. Say, was it really that bad down on the Bong Son Plain?" Everywhere we went, it was the same thing. No one could believe the blood-and-thunder stories, and the motor pool was full of people wanting to see those incredibly battered machines. We even found one rear-area clerk counting the bullet-dings on our turret.

One tank needed a complete suspension rebuild; the crew looked at the task with dread until the battalion motor sergeant came up to the TC and set his mind at rest: "You're back in civilization now Sarge. We handle little things like that up at the shop [meaning battalion maintenance]." He faced toward the shop and gave a hand signal. With that, a pair of giant engines, twelve hundred horses each, rumbled to life and two tank retrievers, ours and the one belonging to Headquarters Company, advanced on the injured tank.

Approaching it from the side, the crews erected the wrecker booms, hooked up lifting slings and, as the awe-struck combat troopers watched, bodily picked it up. The motor sergeant swung both arms down as a signal to the drivers who, moving in concert, drove off carrying their patient into the cavernous depths of the repair shed. Three days later, it emerged from the shop with, as the TC expressed it, new shoes, new legs, and a paint-and-Simonize job.

Overpraising these repair crews would be almost impossible. They never had seen anything like A Company's battered hulls, tracks, and turrets, and they took our "rambling wrecks" as a challenge. After the initial shock, they dug in and ate the problems for breakfast, lunch, and dinner. Working sometimes around the clock while the tankers recuperated, they brought our machines back to a semblance of reliability.

With repairs under control, the company could take a bit of time off for recreation, and Camp Enari had a new feature in U.S. military experience. "Sin City," as it was called, was an authorized government brothel, run by the Army in an effort to control the spread of the virulent strains of Asian VD. Always curious, we had to check this out.

There was no internal connection between the "recreation complex" and the camp, so we couldn't use the base transportation net. We checked out a jeep from the motor pool, and the Ape's crew set out to satisfy our curiosity. As we drove up to the gate, the place looked more like an empty POW camp than anything else. An MP at the gate waved us through, and we checked the place over. The compound contained perhaps a dozen neat, clean, starkly unadorned, one-story buildings. They were of standard Viet construction—woven bamboo walls and thatched roofs that extended out over the porches. They were identical save for a smaller one at the end of the row that displayed the medic's red cross. This, we assumed, was the inspection station.

One thing we knew for certain was that, supervised by

Army MPs and inspected by Army medics, it would be safe; but, like all things controlled by the military, the individuality would be missing.

In an all-too-short two weeks, the company's vehicles had been put to rights, and we were deemed combat worthy and fit to be back at work. This time, instead of searching for companies and battalions of VC, we were to escort convoys at speed over dubious roads, secure villages during their harvest periods, escort medics on rural routes, and bust roads through tropical rain forests. In short, we were to be scattered to the winds again, working in pairs, or teamed up with a PC of infantry or an ACAV (cavalry vehicle). Sometimes we'd simply be given a set of map coordinates and told to go handle the problem. First, however, the company would need its own base camp.

Chapter Nine

CHIO RIO

The carefully lettered sign, painted on a hundred feet of white paper, had been left outside our brand-new company firebase south of Pleiku City. Written in both English and Vietnamese, it read: "WELCOME COMPANY A FROM BONG SON PLEASE LEAVE OUR WOMEN ALONE AND KEEP YOUR DAMN TANKS OUT OF OUR RICE PADDIES."

Lieutenant Walker, now temporarily commanding 1st Platoon, had picked the spot for our new home while the last of the repair work was being wrapped up. Then we cleared out, leaving behind the restrictions of base life (one MP had even given me flak for having rolled-up sleeves).

By the time 3d Platoon arrived at the site, what had been an empty clearing at the side of a dusty, unpaved "highway" was full of the seemingly uncontrolled turmoil of an arriving tank company. The Headquarters combat section (all two of them) had cleared the area and swept it for mines, by having the dozer tank float its blade over the field. Next, the administrative heart and brain of the unit, HQ, supply, mess, and motor sections each picked out a spot, moved their trucks in, and began unloading. Finally, with 1st Sergeant Quinton and Lieutenant Walker directing, the "muscle," or combat platoons, growled into place, creating an iron ring around the softer vehicles. Once the dust settled, the work went on in earnest, because there needed to be at least one ring of concertina barbed wire around the perimeter by nightfall.

As each section of platoon found a spot and set up housekeeping, it was tapped for wire detail. I drew the honor of supervising the mess. First, Top went over the ground with me, and we figured out the exact line of the wire. Then, with a truckload of wire sent along from Battalion, I broke them up into parties, each one responsible for a segment of the wire. Right about here, I got slippery. The truck wasn't due back at Battalion Headquarters at any set time, and driving fence posts is a lot easier from the back of a truck than from the ground. Convincing Top that we would need an extra five-tonner wasn't too hard, and the driver, Sp5 Gray, was eager to experience some of the glamour of life in the rough. As a result, we had a stake-driving platform and the wire went up in record time.

Meanwhile the Headquarters people, using their own labor and what could be spared from wire-stringing (I even went so far as to hide men when I saw another detail forming), pitched their tents and were staking out locations for bunkers. Armored units are always short of manpower, and everybody, including command NCOs and officers, was hauling and sweating. Those of the crews who were left with the tanks were setting tarps and making range cards, getting ready for the night.

Those range cards were a necessary detail. Each tank

used its ranging computer (iron idiot) to designate specific targets and areas of responsibility. This information was kept on a card, which was duplicated in the Old Man's office. That way, one radio call in the middle of the night could bring fire on any suspicious noise or light.

That was one hell of a hard and hectic day, but we all sacked out, except the turret sentries, well satisfied with the progress. The following morning we found that sign in place, and we knew that our reputation, somewhat exaggerated, had followed us. Where they got that bit about the women, I'll never know, but we did have a well deserved rep for destroying real estate and fortifications. We had a good laugh over the incident, and Captain Allen rolled up the souvenir. Then we went back to work, making sure that a more lethal welcome wouldn't catch us unprepared.

Usually there was frantic competition between the combat units to get the hell out of base and gone before the bunker building got underway, but this time we found a way out of that onerous task. The company was assigned a multilingual interpreter named Kim, who was half Montagnard, half Vietnamese. He and My Lin got together and found a village of local Montagnards who wanted to work for us. So we met members of the Rhadé tribe.

The head man in the village came in to dicker over wages, to find out how many men were needed and for what kind of work. What the old fox wanted, it turned out, was an exclusive contract. This was the best thing that could have happened to his tribe, and he wasn't going to let it go by. It would provide employment for his men while the women worked the fields getting in the harvest. After much bargaining back and forth, a mutually satisfactory arrangement was worked out.

The native hill people would, under direction of their head man, take on the KP work of our mess hall, the head

KP carrying a message back to the elder each night, telling him how many extra bodies would be needed for sandbag detail, or whatever, the next day.

My Lin kept her laundry and souvenir "franchise," and we asked the Montagnards to build a bunker for her, along with the regular HQ fortifications. As a fringe benefit, the old man wanted first pickings of our trash and garbage, before it was burned. Once the deal was sealed and the tribal elders came out of the captain's tent with smiles, every Pfc. and Sp4 in the company heaved a sigh of relief—capitalism out in the boondocks had saved them.

While all of the haggling was going on, I remained on the wire-stringing detail, setting the trip flares and explosive booby traps around the perimeter. That was a mistake. The "wheels" in Headquarters were always in need of a detail NCO, one of those people who can be depended on to get results, and not get caught if his methods have to be a little "nonreg." Luckily, 3d Platoon was ready to roll before anyone else, so I was able to get out of there, for a while anyway.

Our first assignment was road security—boring as hell, and the less said about it the better. We would park at an assigned junction or hill crest and look impressive, trying to keep the local VC honest, and hoping some group back in the bush would try something, just to have a piece of action.

"Hey Sarge, look. There's a roof coming down the trail." Holt was lazily scanning the jungle's edge near our temporary strong point, and he'd seen motion where a fairly large trail came out of the foliage to meet what the Viets optimistically called a "highway." Taking the binoculars, I looked, and sure enough, the thatched roof of a Montagnard hut was, apparently of its own volition, coming slowly down the hillside.

A tanker's normal reaction to something strange is to

lay his sights on it. Since Sergeant Hazelip was processing out of the country, and our new platoon sergeant hadn't yet arrived, I was nominally in charge of the Ape. Using the sights, I could now see legs under the mobile thatched roof, so the mystery was solved. The Montagnards practice a slash-and-burn type of agriculture and, since this depletes the topsoil, their houses are built to be moved every few years. We were seeing the first stage of a community move. A dozen men went inside a hut, unlashed the poles, and walked off with the structure. Next would come the walls, then the goods and livestock.

However, the move we were witnessing was of a different kind than usual, and would affect us directly. The VC had been raiding the hill people, killing off entire groups and driving them out of the jungles. It wasn't all one-sided, though; the 'yards are fighters, and those mountains are their home. We saw one complete VC "cell" lying dead on the jungle floor, with crossbow bolts in the backs of their necks.

Now, with their rice harvest due, the Montagnards were in trouble. We couldn't let them fade into the forest, because that would leave the harvest to the Cong. Since guarding thousands of three- and four-family groups would be impossible, and neither their nor our government could afford to arm the people, the only alternative was to bring the families into "fortified hamlets" and truck them, under guard, out to their fields. Since this was a "hurry up" operation, the simplest solution was to park a tank in each group of freshly-moved Montagnards. That way the combat crews could provide night security, and also go about their normal daytime affairs.

In effect each tank or pair of tanks would be living in a stone-age village during the night, with local Popular Forces (about a dozen for foot patrol). During the day we would be expected to make our usual rounds, be it strong point, convoy escort, or shepherding the cross-country medical missions. It was a measure of the Viet Cong in this area that their most common targets were unarmed tribal folk and the U.S. medics who were trying to help them.

Once settled into one of the transplanted villages, the supremely adaptable American GIs began to make new friends and learn new folkways. The Montagnards, for the most part, are a happy, hospitable people. They are easy-going, modest, and, above all, honest. One could forget a wallet or hat on a rock by a swimming hole, and the first of them to come by would track down the owner to return it.

No one, however, could make a play for one of their women. They are much more protective of their honor than most so-called civilized societies—not that these ways are superior, just different. They are also polygamous; the second wife is chosen by the first when she figures the old man is wealthy enough to afford the extra expense and upkeep. The family is the basic unit. When one of the men joined the Popular Forces (Ruff Puffs), the whole family went along with him. I have seen a Puff machine gunner carrying his old Browning, with two wives behind him hauling the tripod and ammo.

Most of the time, our orders would be sent over the tank's radios in the evenings after we had returned to the villages, allowing us to make plans for the next day. This could lead to some strange sights, such as a tank stopping by company base to drop off a half-dozen 'yards, including women, for the medics to work on. I don't think the battalion commander ever quite got over seeing two very pregnant Rhadé women perched demurely on a tank's fenders, as it emerged from company base.

On one occasion, the announcement of a village festival resulted in the ceremonial destruction of a water buffalo yearling by a pair of M48s. The hillfolk believe that the way to ensure tender meat is to beat the animal to death, and the clubbing is part of the preparations for the feast. We had now been part of the settlement long enough to be invited and, being guests, it was only fitting that we should help in the preparations. Not believing in their tenderizing theory and having to escort a section of a truck convoy for a fifty-mile segment of the highway, we came up with a novel method to prepare the meat.

We were to meet the vehicles at 0600 that morning. As we heard the strong points checking off the convoy's progress, Ape cranked up and tore through the settlement's central street at thirty miles per hour, flattening the tethered buffalo in the process, to the cheers of the watching inhabitants. Never having eaten any clubbed meat, I couldn't vouch for that method, but the "tanked" meat was quite acceptable, along with the baked breadfruit, rice cakes, and rice wine.

Let me tell you about that homemade rice wine; it should have been named "Sudden Death" for its potency. The traditional Rhadé drinking ritual didn't help any attempts at sobriety either. In order to properly accept the hospitality of a household, one must drink the wine in a prescribed manner. A long bamboo tube reaching to the bottom of the jug—usually a five-gallon crock—acts as a drinking straw. The head of the house inserts a measuring stick down into the brew, and guests are expected to suck through the straw until the wine has been lowered past the tip of the "meter." So far so good, but stopping for breath is a no-no; it is an insult to his hospitality, and casts doubts on one's manhood. You have to pull it in, in one swell foop! Since only *one* of those drinks could ruin your coordination, we made a point of leaving a sober combat man in each turret.

If the Popular Forces squad leader checking out the immediate vicinity had found no hostiles, the tribesmen would relax, bring out their instruments, and let off some steam. They play a gadget called a string horn—a thick, bamboo tube with strings and sound slots on the sides and a blow tube down the center. When we heard several of these winding up, it was time either to join in, or get back to the tank, depending on the talent of the musicians.

We were living in those camps almost as part of the tribes. Each tank was "adopted" by several families, and we swapped food and sundries with them (GI-issue toilet articles were hot items), and bartered for laundry services. We'd sit around their campfires in the evenings, or in the candle-lit huts if the weather was cool, talking about the Cong, or about America—trying to get words past the language barrier with the help of the Puffs; their rudimentary English helped bridge the gap.

To them, the most fascinating of things were the "American stars" (satellites), and it was a matter of blind faith with these simple people that a nation that could build its own stars would soon rid them of the "night bandits." We didn't see any problem with this line of reasoning, either, because we *knew* we were winning on all fronts, except, as it turned out, on the streets of our own cities. Not one of us believed, back then, that propaganda and ignorance could ever diminish the victories that we bled for.

If the day's work for the section was to guard the workers gathering the rice or corn harvest, we'd show the elders where we would be setting up, and when breakfast was over a silent crew of women and a few Puffs would show up for a free ride to the fields. Once the wicker grain baskets were full, we would help them load up, then bring the rice, corn, and melons in on the backs of the tanks. On one of these excursions, we crushed an eighteen-foot python and, while the women were gathering crops, the men busily turned him into steaks.

Our supper that night was a combination of C rats, rice, snake (which tastes like a cross between fish and chicken), and, believe it or not, watermelon which our cooks had delivered. Since we were eating primarily on the local economy, a lot of the food shipped in for us was either cooked and brought out in insulated cans, or simply dropped off for us to prepare. The Montagnards were intrigued by some of our veggies and fruit, especially watermelon, and there must be some very interesting gardens in those hills by now—they grabbed every seed they could find.

About twice a week we'd be sent out to escort the battalion medics as they made their rounds of the isolated villages. The tribesmen of these settlements had the usual collection of aboriginal ailments—boils, cysts, infections, nutritional defects, dysentery. Our procedure was to use a pair of tanks to escort the medics' M113s and an ACAV carrying an infantry squad and an intelligence officer, with his interpreter.

The tanks would circle a village and sit on the highest point while the infantry and intelligence team checked it out. Then, as the interpreter was asking about recent VC activity, the medics would line up the natives for treatment.

On one of these excursions, a little girl was brought in with a radical dental problem. She was about fourteen years old, and quite pretty, but her left eyetooth had turned forward and was protruding just beside her nose. Her father, the village chieftain, wanted the medics to extract the tooth, but Peterson, the senior medic, took one look and opted for dental surgery.

This meant a trip to Pleiku Air Base, and the medics, through the interpreter, got into a long-winded discussion with the chief. Not only did the old man not want to let his girl go with all those unknown males unprotected, but he wasn't about to trust one of those "wupwups" (helicopters).

So the Ape was diverted to company base, carrying an entire Rhadé family on the back deck, including the grouchy chief, who carried a cocked crossbow and glared suspiciously at everybody in sight.

Unfortunately for us, one of Somolik's section was down for maintenance when we arrived, and he needed another tank for the next morning's convoy. So, as the Montagnard family got into a supply truck for the trip to Camp Enari, we prepared for another grueling run.

Convoy duty was the worst of our highland assignments, not so much because of the occasional ambush, but because of the wear-and-tear on the crews and machines. No one has ever designed a high-speed track for that size combat machine, and the vibration and noise were atrocious. The roads were so badly damaged by mines that, due to wheel-sized holes, the tanks could actually run faster than the trucks. There were no complaints about that, though, as it made it easier to ride herd on the sometimes spooked and nervous drivers.

They all rode with sandbags on the floors of their cabs, weapons at the ready, knuckles white, braced for an explosion. Most of them had a deathly fear of being left behind as stragglers and attacked. Therefore, they would run in an extremely dangerous condition, rather than pull over to relash a load.

"Three-six, this is 3-4 Charlie. I've got a truck with a conex container about to bounce out; request permission to pull him over for relash."

"Roger that, Zippo," Somolik came back. "We're twenty miles out of Chio Rio, so use your own initiative."

"Holt," I said, "pull up alongside him." With tracks clattering to the tune of the laboring diesel, we moved level with the speeding, careening five-tonner. I waved the driver over, nervously watching the wildly bouncing load in the cargo bed. It seemed to be about to go airborne at any minute.

Ignoring my signals, the driver hunched over the wheel, trying desperately to stay in the stream of vehicles. His "shotgun rider" was also staring straight ahead, acting as if nothing was wrong.

"Holt, ease up on him a bit. I'm gonna nail his dumb ass to the wall."

As the tank edged past the truck's front bumper, I swung the Ape's turret to the right and laid the barrel of the ninety on his hood, just in front of the windshield.

"Okay Holt, just slow down gently, pick a level spot, and let's move this sucker off the road."

As the helpless trucker was forced to stop, the "shotgun," a Sp5, stood up in the open cab and started to open his mouth. I cut him off before he could put his foot in it.

"Listen soldier and listen close. There ain't one damn thing you can say without getting in serious trouble. This tank is going to stay and cover you for five minutes only; now get that load strapped down fast!"

"Yes, Sergeant," they chorused. They got to work, and the lashings were repaired before the rest of the serial had gone by. We tagged onto the end of the string, cursing the dumb ass who had forced us into the dust-eaters' position.

One by one, the tanks were feeling the effects of this grueling three-hundred-mile-per-day pace. We were shuttling back and forth between Pleiku, Chio Rio, and Ban Me Thuot, escorting and shepherding trucks, responding to ambushed medics and raided towns. As more of them dropped out for maintenance and repairs, more crews became available for the ones that were still running.

We got a new platoon sergeant who took over the Ape, and at the same time, our company-base ammo sergeant rotated out. There was only one NCO left in the outfit who could handle explosives and had a full knowledge of tanks and their various requirements—me. Sergeant Zumbro's wild freedom came to an abrupt halt one morning, when the Old Man's driver drove up in front of the Ape.

"Grab yer bag, Zippo," the driver said. "The captain's fingered you for ammo sergeant at company base."

Talk about mixed emotions! It was an E6 slot, but I'd spent half a year, or better, with these guys, and these orders made it seem as if I was being kidnapped. The CO's driver, knowing how the tankers felt about base camp, tried to relieve the shock a little.

"It's not like Camp Enari. You know how much time the trucks spend delivering supplies to the combat crews, so you'll still spend most of your time out in the hills; but you'll have a permanent bunk and hot showers."

"Uh huh, that was a good sales pitch," I thought. Saying quick goodbyes to the platoon and the tribal elders, I walked into a new way of life.

Chapter Ten

WHEELIN' AND
DEALIN'

Hey, we got Zippo,'' Dagnall yelled, as I walked up to the tent that housed the ammo section. The Sp5, who I had thought was out in the dozer tank, had taken some grenade fragments and, after returning from the hospital, was reassigned to Headquarters because he was short on time remaining in-country, and was due to go home soon. The rest of that crew of savages were Sp4 Gray, and the company supply clerk, Pfc. Stanley.

The previous ammo NCO had been something of a grump; his personality hadn't fit in with the individuals concerned. Consequently, they had become somewhat demoralized and their effectiveness reduced. Timing is very important in a change of command, even at lower levels such as this. Luckily, I caught them at a good moment: they were depressed, but not rebellious. By this time, I'd earned a reputation and, by treating them decently and setting an example of performance, I got their cooperation.

This was good for everyone concerned, because the war here was heating up. The VC were becoming more active and the traffic on the Ho Chi Minh Trail was reported to be increasing. First Platoon was working east and a bit south of us by then, "opening a new area," as Captain Allen put it. The gates to that piece of real estate must have been very hard to unlock, because they were burning 90mm at a horrendous rate. The ammo section consequently spent most of its time filling crash orders.

The heavy work of stacking and loading was best done early and late in the day, to avoid the tropical heat. My practice was to check at the radio bunker on my way to breakfast to find out if anybody had taken a hit during the night. Then, during breakfast, we could figure out the day's work priorities.

The 1st Platoon, under Lieutenant Walker, who was filling in for another officer, had been shepherding a mixed convoy up from Chio Rio and become involved in a rough one up in the mountains.

When I got the word, they'd been at it all night and, after herding their charges through, were coming in for rest and resupply. Dawn had already broken and it was just before full light when they came over the hill. Three tanks peeled off of the convoy and rolled into the compound, while the other two continued on to Pleiku—"just in case."

The lieutenant jumped down from his tank, jerked a pair of NVA corpses and their equipment off the back deck and dropped them at the tent where the resident intelligence officer lived.

"Two officers for you, Jake," he said, and then, staggering slightly, he disappeared into the command bunker. The rest of the crew, grimed with powder smoke, dust, and exhaust soot until you couldn't tell black from white, headed for the mess hall where we were just finishing our meal.

The Montagnard KPs were already at work. As the men came in they started setting out trays of food, and coffee that the cooks had thoughtfully spiked with brandy.

"What the hell did you get into?" I asked the command tank's gunner.

"Oh man," he said, "that was a royal motherfucker! You know that twisty, narrow section about fifty klicks [kilometers] out?"

We had all been there, so he continued.

"We had a drop-off on one side and trees growing out of the cliffs on the other side. I just knew we'd get hit, because we were running late at night and behind schedule. The first I knew about it was when the gooks dropped out of the trees onto the personnel carrier ahead of us. The lieutenant began giving orders over the radio, and I opened up on the fuckers, trying to avoid shooting into the PC, because it was full of ammo—and the truck ahead of it was a fuel tanker. To make things worse, the next few ahead were full of infantry, and there was hand-to-hand combat going on in those trucks."

Most of us had experienced these panic runs, but this one was starting to sound worse than normal.

"You know, we couldn't button up," he continued, "and it got so bad that one TC took a cannister pellet in the jaw from a backscratching, and a loader on Arapahoe decked an NVA with a ballpeen hammer. The convoy slowed down to a crawl, and a couple of tanks had to push burning trucks off the cliff just to get us moving again.

"After a couple of hours, I had to piss so bad my back teeth were awash, so I grabbed a shell case and half filled it. The lieutenant took the case, and I could see him reaching for his whang too, but the guys on the PC were screaming for more co-ax so we had to get back to work.''

We could all sympathize with him. There are no toilet facilities in a tank, and sometimes after fighting for most of a day, in desperation we'd use a ninety shell case or a helmet, and then just heave it out.

"Walker had missed his aim at the shell case once before, and I thought he'd done it again, 'cause this warm, wet stream came running down my back. I turned around to bitch and . . .''

"Your eyes damn near fell out on your cheeks," the loader cut in. "I'd just spliced another belt into the co-ax, when some shots came through the TC's hatch and bounced around like lead bees. Willie, here, said 'Goddammit, Lieutenant, you're pissi—eeagh!' ''

An NVA had boarded the tank, stuck a carbine into the hatch, and begun firing, trying to kill off the crew. Walker grabbed the weapon with his right hand and, unable to draw from his shoulder holster with his left, he pulled a boot knife and rammed it into the man's jugular vein. The gunner had actually been feeling a stream of blood, running down the lieutenant's arm and pouring off onto his back. The NVA turned out to be an officer, so they packed his remains on the bustle rack, and went on pouring more cannister and H.E. into the underbrush.

When the platoon had broken the ambush and pushed the wrecked vehicles off the cliff, they got moving again—this time, with infantry on the tanks. They were not hit again, so the rest of the run to company base was peaceful—only the sound of engines and tracks disturbing the starry night.

"Yeah, that was a baddie alright," the loader concluded. "Wake me up for supper . . . tomorrow night.''

Eventually we got the delivery method on an even keel, with Gray and two detail men shuttling back and forth between Enari and company base, keeping the bunkers full. We even used Montagnards for this work, which caused a few raised eyebrows around Camp Enari. By getting the convoy schedules and having Gray "hitchhike" with an already escorted group, I eliminated the need for a separate escort. That freed more combat machines from base camp. We always kept a full basic load for one platoon lying in cargo slings on the ground in front of our tent and bunker so that, if somebody got hit, the only delay would be the time it took a chopper to get to us.

But once the load was gone, another sling had to be filled—and fast—because there was no telling whether another platoon, or section, or even an individual tank, would bite into something that bit back. If that happened, I had to find warm bodies in a hurry—moving a half ton of nineties alone is just too damn slow.

First Platoon had taken a hit, and the ready-sling was lifted off. Gray, Dagnall, and Stanley were in Enari with the trucks, and I was getting ready to call Lieutenant Walker for more help, even if he sent 'yard KPs, when he and the CO came out of the command bunker escorting another captain, a lieutenant, and two E7s.

It's an iron rule that the officer in command of a combat situation overrides all nonessential troops, and that he can make use of *any* warm body, regardless of rank. I'd seen the two shiny base-camp jeeps around for most of the morning, and noticed Top and the CO looking bothered.

Captain Allen's dark-brown eyes were now almost dead black. "Zippo," he said, pointing at the two officers and the NCOs, "for the duration of the action, these men are working for you; they've volunteered to help out!"

Yikes, I thought, this is weird. The sling was already in place so, carefully avoiding the impression of giving orders, I said, "I'm gonna need a human chain from me to the cargo net. I'll get in the bunker because I know what and where.'' With that, I dove into the gloom and started pitching out shells and cases.

Once the sling was filled, I dragged my sweating ass out of the bunker, only to hear the Headquarters captain say, ''Well, we're still supposed to inspect your weapons.''

''They're being inspected now by Ho Chi Minh!'' our CO replied.

That comment clarified the situation for me. These people were one of those equipment-inspection teams that came out from base and made a combat soldier's life miserable. We'd even had them drive up to a tank on strongpoint duty to pull a weapons check. Needless to say, the Old Man didn't like this bunch at all, and had been glad for the opportunity to put them to work.

Now, though, it looked as if an argument was about to start. When disagreements arise between high-ranking NCOs and officers, the only place for a buck sergeant is out of sight, so I made myself disappear.

The tanks required fuel and general supplies, as well as munitions, so we set up a three-truck flying column and arranged its schedules to coincide with those of the convoys and off-road patrols. That way we were always escorted. It took some juggling, but it was better than having a fuel-and-ammo truck running around in the heart of a new VC buildup.

To keep things interesting, when one or another of the combat patrols came up with a bunker, or discovered an ammo stash out in the bush, we would have to go blast it. That kept me busy hitchhiking on helicopters and passing tanks, and, in one case, tagging along with an infantry squad that was out looking for trouble and would eventually link up with a tank section. At least I got a chance to run with the tanks for a while, because 2d Platoon's Sergeant Taylor was shorthanded, and I could fill in with his crews until they dropped me off at base.

He had a story to tell about his last convoy escort. The platoon was minus a lieutenant at the time, and he was lead tank for a convoy of general-supply trucks headed for a landing zone west of Chio Rio. They were just about to enter a village, where convoys normally stopped for a maintenance break and where drivers could buy soft drinks from the shopkeepers, when someone noticed that, instead of the usual dozen or so villagers, the only human visible was a little kid squatting on the ground behind a building. His eyes were squinched shut and his fingers were in his ears, obviously bracing himself for a loud noise.

Sergeant "T" had a naturally suspicious nature and, taking the override, he opened up on the dusty street with his co-ax. As the copper-jacketed lead stitched its way through the main drag, one hidden mine after another went off, and the rest of the tanks pulled out of the convoy, coming at full bore. Since their primary mission was convoy safety, and they had no infantry, they proceeded to wreck the main street's houses, and then kept Charlie's head down while the trucks squirted through.

Coming back to the same village, without the trucks, later in the day, they gave the place a good shellacking on general principles. Still without ground troops, they dismounted a few tankers with submachine guns. The village was deserted, the cooking hearths were cold, and almost all personal possessions were gone—another mystery. A few days before, this had been a happy, populated town. . . . Where had all the people gone?

Our chronic shortage of infantry was finally being solved. When I got back to company base this time, there were a couple of new GP tents in the compound, and a half-company was setting up housekeeping.

"More damn mouths to feed," Gray was grumbling. "They got no transport and no ammo section. We'll probably have to supply them, too."

He was right.

"But look at the bright side of it," I said. "All those lovely Pfcs and Sp4s for detail."

He hadn't thought of it that way, and the concept brightened the ammo section considerably.

The foot-sloggers brought another problem with them, though—that Mickey Mouse M16 rifle. With eight years of active duty, much of it airborne infantry, and with a master-rifleman's rating, I state categorically that the "Mattel toy rifle" is not fit for a grown man to fight a war with. Time after time, we'd see the soldiers going out with fully assembled cleaning rods taped to the stocks of their weapons, and the tank commanders had the same disaster story to tell. They would have half a squad out of action at the same time—every one of the soldiers using a cleaning rod or a bayonet to clear the action of his weapon.

Something from way back in the past began to creep to the top of my memory. On one marksmanship detachment, we'd had a couple of instructors—Sergeants Boutin and Vigaletti—who'd shot well enough to have been designated into the United States "President's One Hundred" (the top one hundred marksmen in the nation) for that year. One of them had said something that might explain the problem.

"Brass gets terribly hard when it's compressed, and making cartridges out of it creates brittleness, so each completed case is heated and allowed to cool gradually." He went on to explain, "That's why all military ammo is discolored—to prove that it's been treated."

"Dagnall," I said, "we've got about five different lots

of 5.56mm in the bunker. Get me a couple-hundred rounds of each one, while I go find a rifle.''

I'd been talking quite a bit about this, so when Dagnall showed up with the ammo, there was half an infantry squad with their lieutenant and our Lieutenant Walker, all wanting to see the test. We went to the west end of the perimeter, after warning the troops that there would be a lot of firing—but not to panic; it would all be friendly.

Upon examination, one lot of 5.56 turned out to have nice, shiny case necks, just like civilian ammo. Sure enough, I couldn't get even one magazine of it through a clean, well-oiled M16 without at least three stoppages. Mystery solved: we turned in the bad lot, and that company's blockage rate went down to almost nothing.

The destruction of defective or damaged munitions was another of the section's chores, and this entailed some risk. Because we were usually unescorted, it exposed us to hostile eyes while we were hauling explosives and setting charges. After accumulating a truckload of defective ordnance, we would load it into a 6×6 (very carefully), along with a few hundred pounds of C4, and find a remote area in which to set off a huge blast. Occasionally, I arranged enough time for a swim, so the ground troops could volunteer as escorts for these jaunts.

The prime use of C4 wasn't as an explosive, but for cooking C rations. A golf ball–size lump of the white plastic burned with an intense blue-orange flame, and was the perfect size for a GI's morning ritual. It produced enough heat to boil his coffee, C rations, and shaving water. Since it couldn't be issued without an explosives handler, I found that it was a handy lever for little favors.

Going back to the scene of the previous week's demolitions, we would usually find that Charlie had been prowling through the remains, trying to scrounge something useful. So I decided to see if a ''base-camp commando''

Approaching combat on the Bong Son Plain.

*Apostle just **before** it hit a mine.*

Apostle just after it hit a mine.

Climbing to the central highlands.

Refitting at Pleiku.

Assassin and Lieutenant Somolik going on convoy duty.

Author at the end of the first day of Tet.

Tank and ACAV at the bridge. (The tank has been called out.)

The Ditty Wagon, bane of all high speed traffic.

Tanks and choppers setting up a landing zone west of Pleiku.

Our belly exposed—a nervous time.

Tank moving through a village on the Bong Son Plain.

New dozer tank and VTR hooked up to retrieve a stuck tank.

Our motor section's mascots!

Tank-infantry team returning from patrol.

Author after a day of convoy escort.

could arrange for a few casualties. There were quite a few booby-trap fuses in the inventory so, after stacking the C4 on the pile of defectives, I warned the troops off to a safe distance and rigged M5 antimotion switches and a long delay release—just in case there weren't any customers.

When we got back up the hill, the CO was wondering what had happened, because here I was back—but there'd been no explosion.

"What happened Zumbro, bad fuses?"

"No sir, we booby-trapped this one."

I figured this didn't set well with him, but since just at that moment the charge went off, the Old Man walked back into his tent, mumbling to himself. The man had no sense of humor; I got specific instructions not to try that again—but Top was grinning when he said it.

By Christmas 1967, we knew it had been too quiet in the highlands for too long. All we were able to stir up were sporadic ambushes and night raids, but traffic on the Ho Chi Minh Trail was reputed to be heavy, so we knew the VC were up to something. Just what, no one could guess; all we could do was probe, patrol, and brace ourselves. Christmas, however, is a tradition in the U.S. Army and, unless there is mortal combat going on, most outfits will shut down and celebrate the holidays in the old-fashioned way—with turkey and stuffing, decorations, and the works.

Company A was no exception, and preparations were underway when one of my boys began to show a morale problem. Most of us had received packages from home, and everybody had at least a letter or card from someone. Everybody, that is, but Stanley. During the month or so that we'd worked together, we had become unusually close, and I could sense that something was wrong but couldn't put a finger on it.

Dagnall clued me in. "It's Christmas, and Stan doesn't have anyone. Both his parents are dead, so he's got no one except a sister who was adopted out, and he's lost contact with her."

By a strange coincidence, I had an extra Christmas box. One of my cousins, Bob Addams of Rockford, Illinois, had been in the Korean fracas in '52, and knew about Christmas overseas. He sent a spare "Dear Ralph," and wrote: "In every outfit, there's one poor troop who doesn't get anything for Christmas, so here is his box."

Stanley was just moping around as the rest of us were opening our boxes, so I handed him Bob's card. Then, as he brightened up, almost too surprised for words, I reached under my cot and handed him the package. Stan started to open the present, but his eyes teared up and he said, " 'scuse me fellas," and went off by himself for a while. After he rejoined us, we went on with our holiday celebrations.

In early 1968, I got more and more involved with the functions, machinations, and politics of a base camp. I was getting nervous, because it looked as if I could spend the rest of my hitch here. As the ammo and fuel supply section expanded its scope to cover a widely scattered company and its auxiliaries, our contacts at Battalion Headquarters and Camp Enari increased, and by accidentally filling a vacuum, we found ourselves in several businesses—one of them quite illegal.

Each company was issued a certain amount of beer, and could buy a certain amount over quota; but that was strictly regulated. Down on the plains, there was no problem. As long as there was a local supply, we just bought it from the locals. But up in the highlands the villages were fewer and more scattered, so the crews needed a better supply. After all, the water wasn't safe, so why take unnecessary chances.

Since we had the dubious honor of making the beer run, some subtle pressure was put on us to find ways to increase the supply. (If there was a tank available, it would be waiting outside Enari's main gate to act as a personal escort for the beer truck.) There was more than enough on the loading docks, and a small collection was taken up to provide enough to buy extra, and to convince the Vietnamese foreman to move a few decimal points on his records. In addition, My Lin made contact with one of the Viet stewards at the base officers' club, so every week one of the drivers would pick up a few cases of hard liquor.

After the first few loads, the whole thing snowballed. The demand got so large that we were actually operating a small-scale gray market, and it was getting to the stage where a few palms would have needed greasing if we were to continue to operate. We were trying hard to figure a way out of a situation that could get very sticky, when Uncle Ho took a hand in our affairs again.

Chapter Eleven

DOWNTOWN
PLEIKU—TET 1968

For weeks we had been hearing horror stories coming out of Pleiku. My Lin reported large groups of Viet Cong moving into entire neighborhoods, and the barracks maids in Camp Enari told of murders in the city as communist cells forced their will on the people.

Gray, back from a supply run, described the changed atmosphere in the city: "Zippo, the whole place is tense, and there's a lot more of those military-age males around. Arrogant little bastards, too; they look you over like they were measuring you for a coffin."

Snipings had increased radically, and raids near the Cambode border had expanded to the point where A Company's particular brand of expertise was needed. Captain Allen passed the word, and we were in the process of dismantling our private firebase when Sergeant Quinton buttonholed me.

"Third Platoon is temporarily assigned to defend Pleiku Air Base. They'll probably be there for quite some time, so I want you to take some trucks and set them up with an ammo dump. Better take your gear," he said, grinning at my obvious pleasure, "the job may take a while."

Dagnall was rotated out, and Stanley, with my recommendation, found a home in a 1st Platoon tank. My new driver, Richardson, was a good man. He, Gray, and I loaded up a selected list of packaged nastiness, and headed for the air base—anticipating a spell of Air Force luxuries. Our relatively unfettered life out in the bush had its advantages, but we'd heard rumors of an air-conditioned NCO club on the base and we were eager to check it out.

Approaching the base entrance, we could see why they were having problems. Their only defenses were a single-apron barbed-wire fence that a kid with a boy-scout knife could have opened up, and, about every fifty or hundred yards, guard towers that looked like Crackerjack boxes.

"We're looking for part of Company A, 1st of the 69th," I told the AP at the gate.

"Ain't no Army on the base."

"Well what made those," I asked, pointing down at tread marks, "a centipede?"

"Oh, you're with the tanks," he said with a laugh. "Just follow this road, take the left fork, and stop before you run over the brass."

"What brass?" I asked.

"Damn near every flight officer is down at the warehouse where your tanks are parked, scoping those big mothers out."

That, I thought, wouldn't please Lieutenant Joe. After living with the barely-housebroken savages of 3d Platoon, he'd come to share our distrust of higher-echelon command and their lack of originality. The AP was right; the hulls and turrets were swarming with curious pilots, and the lieutenant was talking with a pair of bird colonels.

Climbing out on the truck's hood, I cupped my hands and hollered, "Hey Lieutenant, where do I dump the explosives?" This drew a few black looks from the assembled "wheels," but an Air Force sergeant detached himself from a group of tankers and came over with a dozen airmen.

"We'll put your loads in the bomb dump," he said, "and these warm bodies are yours as long as you need 'em."

As his troops were unloading the trucks, while my specialists supervised the stacking, he brought me up to date. "We simply don't have the manpower to defend the perimeter of an air base. The runways make it so huge that even a battalion of infantry couldn't do the job. Consequently, we've been getting penetrated fairly often, and last night the Cong got into the revetments, blew a fighter to scrap, and killed the ground crew. Our general asked yours for some help, and the next thing we knew, those iron monsters of yours were coming through the gate."

After the trucks were emptied, I sent my two specialists and their Air Force work detail back for more ammo and the Air Force sergeant took me, and the rest of 3d's noncoms, for a fast tour of the base—ending at that fabled, air-conditioned club. What a change in lifestyle! We had Air Force chow, hot showers, the NCO club, PX store, movies, and women—for one evening.

At 0400, the shit hit the fan. One of those undersized VC battalions, about six hundred of them, cut the wire, blew out three machine-gun towers, and came on the airstrip in a dead run headed for the revetments and hangars. However, they didn't know the tanks were there, and that made all the difference. Trusting nobody else's security, the crews slept in and on the tanks, with someone at the gun controls twenty-four hours a day. So when the towers went up, eight iron murder machines were moving before the flames died out.

I'd been helping Lieutenant Somolik and his crew pull watch and, when the music started, I hit the ground and ran for the ammo dump. My buddy, Sergeant Hiemes, gave a wave and a yell as he and the dozer tank led the column out. The Avenger was next, followed by the 3d Platoon, and a stray from 1st Platoon that had been at company base for repairs.

Talk about a field day! What a target for machine guns and 90mm cannister—close-packed enemy on a runway. About an hour later, the tanks were coming in for ammo, the crews jabbering like crazy men, with airmen hanging all over the hulls—all talking at once.

Later, we pieced together what happened. The tanks rolled down the taxi lane between the hangars and the fighter revetments (the ground crews were sleeping around their planes with Ml6s); then they cut across the runway and, on signal, turned ninety degrees and charged the Cong flank in line abreast. About one hundred yards from the nearest hostile, they switched on the searchlights— seventy-five million candlepower each—and let go with full armament. Right then, the ground crews opened up and the remaining guard towers proceeded to beat up the VCs' rear. There were over two hundred bodies on that airstrip, and blood trails going back through the wire.

For the next few days, we were celebrities. It seemed as if everyone on the base, from airman 1st on up through fighter pilot and wing commander, wanted a guided tour of a tank and, if possible, a ride. In return, we were taken on tours through fighters and given rides in dragon ships. In the clubs, as soon as we ordered, the nearest airman hauled out his wallet to buy us drinks and food. The fly-boys had really been bothered by those raids, and they thought we were the best thing since horse cavalry.

Lieutenant Somolik had taken to going out on patrol at 0300, running on infrared lights, and quite a few Air Force men were hitching rides to see how we worked. There had been some snipings, but nothing serious, and I'd had enough of base life. The ammo bunker was organized, and my Sp5s were a responsible bunch, so one fine morning I hitched a ride with Somolik in the Assassin, too. That morning was the beginning of the Vietnamese New Year— Tet.

0200: A voice attached to a shadowy shape woke me up with a canteen cup of coffee and a mess kit (real—not C rations) full of scrambled eggs, bacon, and burned toast. The coffee had a heavy load of sugar and Crown Seven— it pulled me awake really quickly. We checked out the tank, including tightening the track end connectors, all three hundred twenty of them.

0300: Roll-out. The air-base CO had made a rear gate out of the hole the VC had left in the wire. We went out at fifty-yard intervals, spread into a rough wedge, and headed for our first checkpoint—a commo relay station on a ridge east of Pleiku. The lieutenant had a full crew, so I rode shotgun, perched on the turret and hanging onto the top-mounted fifty caliber (as a combat modification, we had welded machine-gun mounts to the turret).

The loader, Bronco Kindred, had been a driver the last time I'd seen him, but the lieutenant had switched him from the Apostle to eliminate friction between him and the new tank commander. The gunner, an E5 sergeant named Wally, was a new man, and the driver was a Fort Hood-trained recruit—green, but willing.

0430: Rolling up to the relay station, Lieutenant Joe and I went in to check the place out, and to scrounge coffee for the crews. The CO there, a Signal Corps lieutenant, was an easygoing type who wanted us to convoy a busload of USO people back as far as Pleiku City. The entertainers, a Philippine country-western band and two Australian strippers, had spent the night rather than chance an ambush after dark.

The signals lieutenant, a tall freckle-faced kid, had a story to tell about that. It seems that the strippers had volunteered to go all the way with the station men, but couldn't because General Stone was supposed to be stopping by on a helicopter inspection tour. So the commo techs conjured up a fake mortar raid. They stationed a man outside the radio bunker with a sack of concussion grenades and every time there was any communication with the general's chopper, he would heave two or three over the wire for effect. The general, very concerned, cautioned them to take no chances with the girls and stayed away. Everybody was chuckling as the troupe's bus fell in behind the Ape.

0600: Approaching the outskirts of Pleiku, we began hearing small arms and light mortars from downtown. Captain Allen cut in on the radio saying that a North Vietnamese Army main-force battalion was occupying the downtown area, and we were instructed to "probe" for information.

0615: We met two ARVN M41 tanks coming out of the city in full retreat. They looked very natty, men wearing black berets, turrets polished—they were also scared shitless; you could see the whites of their eyes at one hundred yards. They told of RPGs and B40 rockets being fired out of trees and windows. They said the NVA was disorganized because they were actually parts of two battalions that had been thoroughly mauled, and were trying to regroup.

On hearing this, Captain Allen called off the probing and said, "Just go in there, link up with our infantry, and hash them up.'' The ARVN were glad to escort the USO group to a safer zone, and we spread out and rumbled into town.

0700: First, there wasn't any U.S. infantry. We were it—eight tanks with a few Air Force hitchhikers; about forty of us against an NVA main-force battalion. Tanks and infantry have been a functioning team since the Battle of Cambrai in 1917, and going into a built-up, infested area without grunts caused us acute distress. Without ground troops, we had to go in with the hatches open and our heads out. Since I was supernumerary, I took an M3 grease gun, braced myself in the loader's hatch, and stayed out of Bronco's way.

We were on a main street south of the business district, when we began taking heavy fire, mostly small arms, but with some .50 caliber and mortar mixed in. Somolik eye-balled the size of the NVA infection, expanded our line to match it, and we moved in. Halfway through the turn, the 1st Platoon tank took a rocket under the bow and a wicked blast of LMG (light machine gun) fire. The driver was killed; the loader was swept off the turret by MG fire; the tank commander was blown out of his hatch; and the gunner, Stanley, was burned, but came out under his own steam, cussing a blue streak.

All he'd ever wanted was to be a tanker and, since he had worked his butt off for me handling ammunition, I had wangled a slot for him in that tank. He low-crawled down the road about twenty yards, where the 6-tank, commanded by Cheyenne Black, called to him and took him aboard.

Just then, someone came on the air and said, ''We're taking fire from that ARVN compound.''

Captain Allen, back at base camp, came in with, ''Well, blow it away, too.'' The captain was as busy as a one-armed paperhanger because he had one platoon in combat, one convoying trucks down to Chio Rio, and one setting up a new company base camp. While he was not known for innovative tactics, he *did* have the standard GI reaction to a bad situation—raw, brutal attack.

0730: Somolik detailed Ape and Avenger to that chore. They peeled off the end of our line and charged the earth berm that surrounded the compound. The fortification wasn't designed to stop tracked vehicles, so they roared up and over it, going in blind—guns flaming almost continuously.

"Do you need any help?" the lieutenant asked, anxiously.

"Negative," answered Sergeant Rodriguez, the new platoon honcho, his voice almost inaudible above the racket of gunfire and a full-bore engine. "We're rompin' and stompin' in here, and they'll be coming over the wall in a few minutes."

His estimate was accurate. NVA shortly swarmed over the south wall, only to fall victim to Black in the 6-tank, who took them in the flank with a combination of co-ax and .50 caliber. The two 3d Platoon tanks came up on the defensive wall and, balancing like vultures, finished off the fugitives with cannister.

0800: By now, some infantry were filtering in; they were Montagnard Popular Forces, the Puffs, led by a Special Forces A-team. They weren't used to working with tanks, but after the SFs gave them a short briefing, they divvied up, attaching themselves to individual tanks.

We punched our way through a city block of houses and gardens until we took heavy rocket fire. The dozer tank took a hit in the turret and was blowing black smoke. The crew went back to where the battalion recon platoon was organizing a command post. Somolik was going to shift tanks to cover the hole, but a new voice came over the radio net.

"Chopper 36, this is Black Watch Niner. I'll fill your gap." Lieutenant Joe and I glanced at each other in disbelief as a Huey gunship settled into the hole left by the dozer tank. He lasted almost two minutes in the heavy fire, then, exclaiming, "Jesus Christ, it's hot down here!" he lifted out and vanished. (My suspicion was confirmed in '81 when I met a pilot who had been in this battle. That gunship operator was a bachelor.)

0900: A Special Forces sergeant came up to tell us that the NVA had not run the civilians off; they were tied up in the houses from which the MGs were firing. As we pulled back to figure this one out, some U.S. infantry showed up. I'll never know where they came from—no trucks, no APCs, nothing. They just materialized. Somolik went with a radioman to find their CO, leaving us with orders to sit tight and fire on "targets of opportunity." Knowing him, that meant mill around, shoot up the enemy, but don't wander off.

After a brief discussion, Sergeant Wally ceded his command to me. (It was his tank, but he'd been in-country for only three weeks.) We found ourselves a low spot that afforded some protection and scanned the area. Just as we were going to try a long shot at that ex-ARVN compound, an Air Force spotter came on the net, described a building, and asked who could hit it. We could.

He said that he had seen a dozen hostiles enter it, and he would drop white phosphorus for a positive mark. As soon as the smoke appeared, we drilled 90mm high explosive delay into the building's foundation—the idea being to blow the floor out through the ceiling. But on the eighth shot the gun jammed! Bronco almost gave himself a hernia trying the extractor, but that shell wouldn't go in or out.

This, I thought to myself, is what you get for glory—guess whose job it was to do it the hard way. We swung the turret so the gun tube pointed over the right rear, away

(I hoped) from most enemy fire. With Wally and Bronco watching for trouble, I eased out, dropped down, and grabbed hardware out of a sponson box. I had to assemble the rammer staff, which is a giant cleaning rod, put a bell rammer on it, and pound that cursed cartridge out backwards. While I was doing this, Bronco took the time to clear out the empties, heaving the ninety hulls before the clutter could jam the traverse gear.

As all of this was going on, a Green Beret and a couple of Puffs showed up and gave me a bit of security. The sergeant admitted that he had always wanted to try the armored battalions, but was rapidly changing his mind. As I put the rammer away, Bronco heaved the last batch of empties out—along with a case of Budweiser empties, some still cool.

I called out, "Hey Wally, give me some cold ones, will ya," and they came sailing out the hatch. We drank to each other's health; then the Beret took his Puffs down the road while I got back to work.

If it wasn't one thing, it was another. Just as we got straightened out, the 6-tank had its left track shot up. With one tank burning and exploding, and one disabled and abandoned, we were beginning to thin out. Only four tanks were still hammering the NVA positions, so I rolled Assassin up to Cheyenne's cripple and put two men in the turret to provide cover.

1030: We managed to get enough spare track sections together and reassembled Black's running gear. By this time, I had established a commo link to the air base, and one of the recon tracks had gone to escort in my ammo trucks. Captain Allen withdrew 2d Platoon (Sfc. Taylor commanding) from a convoy staging area and, operating on information from Lieutenant Somolik, sent them into town from the west end. Taylor effectively smashed the NVA defensive line by hitting its exposed flank with two-hundred-fifty tons of bad news—doing what tankers do best: shoot, scoot, and communicate. He also solved the problem of those civilians by taking out the gunners with his tracks—smashing them to a pulp.

1130: With 2d Platoon engaged and my ammo section coming in from the north, it was time to pull back and rearm. Fortunately, Somolik had shown up with the infantry CO and was back aboard, because I was about to get really busy.

As we backed away from the action, the driver, a kid we called Chubby, came over the intercom. "There's some clown in civvies with a shotgun coming in from the left." Lo and behold, it was the local Catholic missionary priest.

"What're you doing, Padre?" asked the lieutenant.

"Looking for the sonofabitch that blew up my school. Can you help the mission compound? It's under fire."

"Sure thing, Padre, and if you'll wait a while, we'll get you an infantry squad."

The priest replied, "Thanks soldier, but I know where he lives and it's personal." He walked off with his double barrel and we never saw him again.

Somolik reached the 6-tank on the radio, and sent Black and a recon APC to pry the nuns and nurses loose. Later, Stanley told me, "Darnedest thing I ever saw, Sarge. We demolished the wall, swung left, and made room for the track. I got out to look around and here's about a half-dozen broads with suitcases, looking like they were waiting for a bus. They were all half-looped and this little Vietnamese nun handed me a pint martini—with a cherry in it. They loaded up on the track and we all got out of there. Recon took the women out and we went over to your resupply point."

1215: My two crazies, Gray and Richardson, had managed to get separated from their armored escort, so they just drove their ammo trucks toward the sound of tank guns, stopping when they ran into U.S. infantry. A squad leader radioed their position to us. From what we could see on the map, it looked good, so the lieutenant withdrew our little task force to the plaza that the drivers had picked, set up security, and began to restock the tanks. Several tanks, as they came in to refill, turned out still to have one or two hitchhiking Air Force men on board taking up the slack where crews were short. They rode in empty gunner's seats or filled in as impromptu loaders.

Now that the war was catching up with us again, they were getting some unexpected O.J.T. (on-the-job training), and like veteran tankers they joined in the shell handling. Awestruck, they made comments such as, "Man, you guys take this personal." One man said, "You know, you can really express yourself with one of these things. I think I'll change services next hitch." Only Americans can adapt to a change like that, and come up fighting.

1300: Once I had the resupply operation working smoothly, with two tanks at a time rearming and four holding a perimeter (one was with the infantry, busting strong points), Somolik took me aside.

"Sarge, you were airborne infantry weren't you?"

"Yes sir, what did you have in mind?"

"Well, we've got one body to find and the dozer to check out. Bronco was a tunnel rat down south, and I figure that, between the three of us, we could get it done while the crews load up."

Bronco had one of those three-shot M79s; the lieutenant had his Car-16; and I had the usual M3 and a .45 automatic. We eased down the street to the point where we'd originally been hit, and found a platoon of ground troops, part of an A-team, and about a dozen Puffs mopping up.

A rifle bullet cracked just over our heads and we pulled back quickly, taking shelter behind a low wall. "One more for that turkey," a squad leader said, motioning to one of his men. The detailed soldier walked slowly out into the open, acting as if he didn't know about the sniper. He took two steps forward, then instantly snapped back as a bullet zipped through the space he had occupied. Immediately, a burst of machine-gun fire tore into the window from which the NVA was firing.

"Third one today," the squad leader announced proudly. "They never seem to learn to move after a couple of shots, so we just sucker them into revealing themselves."

"Now that takes balls," Bronco said. Coming from an ex-tunnel rat, it was high praise indeed.

We found the loader's body in a ditch, covered with debris; it was roughly fifty feet from his tank, which was still burning. After making arrangements with the infantry to remove his body, we tried to get to the dozer tank. We found out really fast that an NVA machine gunner still had it under observation. It didn't appear to be badly damaged; most of the smoke was coming from external supplies and gear.

Crawling out of there on knees, elbows, and bellies, we marked the MG position for future attention, and got back to the ammo point. When we arrived, the battalion CO, Colonel Riggs, who was up in a chopper, got on the lieutenant's case over the radio.

"Choice Shopper 3-6, this is Big 6, there's three of your tankers running around loose down there; get them rounded up before they get killed!"

Somolik, appearing a bit worried, replied, "From up there, how can you tell that it's tankers?"

"Do you know anyone else that would be wearing cut-off fatigues, jungle boots, and bandoliers instead of shirts?"

"No sir."

"Well then, round up those three savages and put them back in their cans."

The lieutenant gave me a lopsided grin and said, "Yes sir—out."

1430: With 3d Platoon loaded up, the 2d was trickling back for more shells and a breather. Somolik stayed around long enough to relay info on the dozer tank to Sfc. Taylor, and then took his tanks back into the fight. I got 2d replenished, then received orders to move the supply point over to the command post to supply the recon tracks and the infantry.

1530: After we got consolidated in the remains of the ARVN compound, what should suddenly materialize but a dozen unescorted, unannounced munitions trucks from Camp Enari. Some genius in Division Headquarters had decided we didn't know enough to order resupply on our own. The trucks were crammed with goodies normally in short supply, so I put my bandits to work and we rearranged some loads—you don't look a gift horse in the mouth.

1600: Sergeant Taylor, who always had a flair for the dramatic, came in with the dozer tank. After silencing that pesky MG, he had rounded up Sanchez and Kennet (the remains of the crew), "injuned" up behind it, jumped aboard, and had driven off with it. The turret was a bloody mess. A rocket had hit one of the armored window's slits and the spray of armor glass had literally sheared off the commander's skull level with his ears. I helped haul the body out, and we added him to a growing line of blanket-draped bodies at one side of the compound.

1700: I'd just finished organizing the spare trucks and surveying the dozer (it also had taken some hull damage, and was leaking fuel and transmission oil), when Somolik and his crew came back for more 90mm cannister and some demolition gear.

"You better get the trucks out of here, Sarge," Lieutenant Joe told me. "There's likely to be mortar and rocket fire until we dig out their artillery section."

"Yes sir, this dozer's pretty well fucked up, and Sanchez and Kennet are in a blue funk."

"Well, take it with you; if it can be fixed, it's yours. Captain Allen will confirm the post, and, anyhow, you need to be out of base camp before you get busted."

"Yes sir!"

Second and 3d Platoons went on to set up a night laager. I took Executioner and those extra ammo trucks, along with my two, and headed back to the air base, taking care not to stand in the blood-spattered cupola.

I didn't really want to crowd a crew that had just lost a boss who was also their buddy, so for the next few days, I just worked on the transmission leak and hauled supplies and munitions. Finally, with the NVA on the run and the company beginning to slow down, the crew started to unwind.

"Thanks for not coming on too strong," Kennet said, as he scraped the last of the blood-specked gray matter from the inside of the commander's cupola. "I don't think I could have done this job right off the bat."

I was busy replacing the armored window, and just let him and Sanchez talk until they got it out of their systems.

The dozer, with triple the normal mileage on it, was sort of a rambling wreck—but I'd been there before and could work with it. The blade pump was scragged; the engine and transmission were swapping oil; and the tracks were worn to the point that some blocks had to be removed to tighten them. The road wheels were leaking grease from worn seals and several torsion bars needed to be replaced. Other than that, though, the old girl was in pretty good shape.

Chapter Twelve

LIFE WITH THE ENGINEERS

Officially, the two Headquarters tanks belonged to the Old Man and the exec, but in this war those officers had to spend more time in helicopters than on the ground. So those two machines were used as an extra light section, and as temporary replacement vehicles to fill platoons that had one down for repairs.

After reporting that the transmission leak was under control, and that the crew had quit vibrating from their loss, my new boss, Cheyenne Black, got on the radio.

"We're assigned to provide security for a group of engineers clearing a road south of Pleiku." He fed me a reference point and a string of numbers for a rendezvous point. Then we took off. Those reference-point designations were necessary because the Cong captured quite a few American radios, and a location in "clear" numbers would have been asking for an ambush.

The dozer, Executioner, was a known personality because of the extra tonnage on its bow. Since we were rolling past our old base, we received many waves and smiles from the Rhadé and the Vietnamese who lived in the region. Cruising at a comfortable twenty miles per hour, we passed the location of our old company base; it was still being picked over by scavengers. Down the road was our old "borrow pit," where I'd supervised so many sandbag details. It was a pleasure to get waves and cheers from "our" Montagnard village, now secured with barbed wire and defended by its own Puffs.

The countryside was so beautiful and picturesque that any minute I expected to find a *National Geographic* camera crew instead of patrol vehicles. During this period, I had the time to think about what my preparations had been for this kind of war, and how far off base some of them had been.

Stationed in Germany for a few months before shipping to Nam, I'd been studying and practicing gunnery and tactics. Several budding tank commanders among us met an old Afrika Korps tanker who had fought under Rommel in World War II. Listening in awe, we heard Willie spin tales of the great armored battles of that war. Unfortunately, nothing in his stories helped us with the battles we were facing in the jungles and hamlets of Vietnam. The Germans didn't have to use tanks for hand-to-hand combat.

My cousin, Barry Doyle, had been a tanker in Korea, and some of his experience helped. There, the Shermans sometimes were used for bunker-busting and village combat, and Barry gave me a few tips such as how to use the .50 to flush people out of semihard buildings, and how not to make sharp turns in paddies. He also warned me not to expect much accuracy from jets in ground attack. He said, "They're just too fast for accurate bombing.'' Much of his advice, however, was for use against tanks, and didn't apply to our type of combat.

I was thinking how unique this war was, with far-flung commands fighting independently, yet linked closely by radio, artillery, and choppers, when Kennet's voice interrupted my reverie.

''There's Widowmaker under that tree on the right up ahead.'' Picking up the binoculars, I could see the telltale belch of oily-black smoke, as the diesel rumbled to life and the 6-tank rolled out into the sun.

In an effort to cut back on ambushes which were the bane of the truckers' existence, Division Command had the engineers clear a two-hundred-yard-wide swath on either side of the more heavily traveled roads in the highlands. With Rome plows on the D8 Caterpillars, the machines became giant brush cutters that could also double as tree-felling equipment. These blades were asymmetrical, with long, pointed spikes on one side, tapering back to giant sawteeth that had to be sharpened with power grinders each night.

The Viet Cong, what remained of them after the Tet disaster, did not like this at all, and were sniping at and ambushing the engineers as they worked. Cheyenne chuckled over the radio, as he gave me the dope on their problem. We knew both the words and the tune to that song, and the snipers would be dancing to livelier music than they bargained for.

''Hey Zumbro,'' one of the engineer sergeants called out, as we pulled up and parked. ''I see you finally got out of company base.''

Now who in the hell knows me way out here, I thought.

''Remember when my section of orphans came to A Company, tired and hungry?''

''Oh yeah,'' the memories came back to me. This guy

had been out on his own with a section of earthmovers, two front loaders on lowboys, and a pair of dump trucks, and had been about as tired and demoralized as a person could get, when he came through the gate. His assignment had been to travel from one firebase to another, performing whatever earthmoving jobs the local commanders had wanted done.

The Old Man had warned me there was an engineer crew on the way, since I was handling the firebase detail, ammo and fuel section, so I took them under our wing. When they'd come through the wire, there'd been hot chow waiting, the wood-burning showers were warm, and we'd given them a case of beer. Dagnall had found a projector and some "blue" movies, and after chow we'd invited them over for a show and some more beer. They'd seemed shocked, and the next morning the sergeant had told me why.

"Nobody has rations allocated for extra bodies, so we've been eating Cs while other troops get hot chow. Not only that, some outfits make us stand guard with their own troops after we've reworked their fortifications. It just ain't fair, and we were just about to radio in to our CO and ask for recall."

"Well," I remember asking, "can you stay a day or two, and give us a hand?"

He stretched, grinned, and answered. "I talked it over with the boys last night after showers. This outfit of yours lives up to its reputation, and your hospitality is the next best thing to R&R. Where do you want us to move this part of Asia to?"

They had stayed with us for most of a week back then, and now as we climbed off the tanks he said, "It's our turn. So come with me and check out an engineer mess hall."

Man, these guys knew how to live in a war zone! The

mess hall was built into a five-ton truck, and they had a GP tent with tables and chairs—just like at a base camp. Their machines were maintained by powered shops-on-wheels, and their generator truck powered an air-conditioned "company club" in a tent. For hot showers, they put an immersion heater in a water trailer and heated the whole damn six hundred gallons. Not only did our section live high on the hog for those few weeks, but we were able to get a lot of repairs done on the tanks.

With their welding equipment, we got our fenders repaired, bustle racks reworked, and had extra machine-gun mounts put on the tops of the turrets. I'd scrounged up an extra co-ax, and they welded a bow-gun mount for me, so we could have a fixed, forward-firing gun just behind the dozer blade. We had new torsion bars flown in, and they swapped them, using powered equipment, in half the time it would have taken us to do it.

They'd been taking sniper damage so, each morning after a leisurely breakfast, our section would go out on patrol, circling their work area in a random search pattern—sometimes stopping one vehicle, while the other made noise. At other times, we would use the sound of the working dozers to mask the sound of our running, and would literally sneak up on an unsuspecting bunch of would-be snipers.

We'd long since memorized the maps, and probably knew the terrain better than the local VC. Using this knowledge, one of the tanks would run ahead of the work party, using passing trucks or aircraft to mask the sound of the tracks; then we'd shut down and wait. Once we even put a dummy in the loader's hatch and sat out in the open, hoping for some sniper to take the bait; we had no luck on that one, though—the word was getting around.

Occasionally, we would separate, working opposite

sides of the road, or taking both sides of a hill at the same time. On one of these runs, I heard Black's co-ax open up for a short burst.

"Trouble?" I asked anxiously, over the radio.

"Nope," he replied. "Supper." When they came around the hill and out into the open, a small deer was draped across the turret.

With deer, wild pig, and the tasty peacock-pheasants, we enjoyed a variety of game to supplement the issue rations. The engineers had made a giant charcoal cooker out of a fifty-five-gallon drum, and they would roast wild game at the drop of a hat. Once, a combination of circumstances led to a large fish fry.

The engineers had inadvertently blocked a stream with brush and dirt, forming a pond behind it. The tanks, trying a new trick, were coming down the same creek, using the water to keep the tracks from rattling. By the time we reached the base of the hill, the tracks had driven most of the fish out of the stream and into the pond.

"Hey, are you thinking what I'm thinking, Zippo?"

"You bet, Sanchez. It's gonna be fish-fry time. Kennet, back this sucker up on the bank so I can get a little depression."

Dropping the muzzle, we let off an H.E.P. round, and the water exploded with fish—all over the bank, into the bushes, up on the tank, even into the open turret hatches. In our eagerness, we had gotten a bit too close, and now we were slipping in a flopping mess of fish. We finally got them bagged up and ourselves washed off, and headed for the mess hall.

Life wasn't all a bed of roses. The sniping never did quite stop, but it was reduced sharply and the engineers took far fewer casualties. Also, there were a few noncombat hazards in the jungle—such as snakes. In addition to the cobra, there was one especially nasty customer known as the Bamboo Viper. Blending in with the tropical foliage, it is greenish yellow in color, and hangs on branches to drop onto its prey. It has a nerve toxin; the GIs called it "Step-and-a-half" because that was about as far as one could go after being bitten by it.

There was also a particularly vicious kind of stinging, red, tree ant that lived, like paper wasps, in hanging nests; the slightest tap from a tank hull was sufficient to drop the nest into a hatch. One visitation from a colony of these ants was enough to evict an entire crew, and create in them the habit of nervously scanning the trees ahead.

Even with the snakes and ants, it was relatively easy duty, after downtown Pleiku. But all good things must come to an end. One day a new pair of tanks showed up to take over security, because the road was now in another division's area of responsibility. As usual, our company was busy, spread out, and we were needed.

Hostile activity was increasing west of Camp Enari, and the Viet Cong with reinforcements from the NVA had, as one of their principal targets, the bridges on Highway 19 West out to the Cambode border. Highway 19 East, going down to the coast by way of An Khe and Qui Nhon, was already garrisoned in part by our 1st Platoon. The decision was made to stretch the company out to the limit—all the way to the western border.

The transmission leak in the dozer tank had finally stabilized at about a quart an hour, and the seals between the engine and the trannie were gone. So, instead of having thirty-weight oil in the engine and ten-weight in the transmission, we had an average of twenty-weight wandering around in there. After requisitioning three five-gallon cans from the engineers, I said goodbye to my friends, and trailed along behind Widowmaker, setting off for the new company base.

A bit north of Camp Enari was a giant, ridgebacked hill known to the natives as "Dragon Mountain." As we approached it, anticipating the shade of its forested base, our orders were changed. We were temporarily rerouted to pick up and escort a trio of supply trucks destined for the new company firebase. Something new had been added, we noticed, as we entered Enari's main gate.

"You have to check your weapons and ammo here at the station," the MP corporal told Black.

Cheyenne Black, as ornery-looking a battle sergeant as had ever been set in a turret, glared down at the kid and said, "Sure, sonny. Where do you want me to park it?"

"What do you mean, Sarge?"

"There's so damn many weapons in here that, if you tried to give me receipts for them, you'd be here all day. And the tank, itself, is a weapon so you've accomplished nothing but block traffic."

"But . . . but . . . my orders—"

"Get out 'n the damn road boy. I got no time for your foolishness!" And with that, Widowmaker rolled past the unfortunate kid who, giving up, walked disconsolately back into his gate bunker.

In the hour the supply people took to get the loads on the trucks, we managed to snag a jeep and trailer and make it to the PX, the NCO club, and a few other places, restocking the "necessities." Finally, with the trucks in tow, we headed for the gate again. This time, an MP lieutenant was standing by the corporal's side, and he looked pissed.

Black, who was leading our miniconvoy, gave me orders. "I'm going full bore, Zippo. Can your transmission take it?"

"Yeah," I said, "for a minute or so."

"Okay, keep it closed up and follow my lead."

Tanks can raise an unbelievable amount of dust, and we swept through the entrance like a young whirlwind. All that the MPs saw was a dusty cloud from which issued a pair of barely audible "good afternoon sirs," accompanied by two dust-shrouded salutes.

The new firebase was an earth-bermed, wire-topped compound sitting (for once) on level ground. After we found parking places and had taken care of our crews and vehicles, Lieutenant Walker sent for us.

"There have been some changes," he said. "For one thing, Captain Allen was shifted to staff, and we've got a new CO, Capt. John Biggio.

"The tactical situation has changed," he went on to tell us. "The VC are pretty well whipped as a military force after Tet, but the Ho Chi Minh Trail is still going full bore, and the North Vietnamese are sending regiments down it. We're only a few miles from the border, and the remaining VC are trying to keep the bridges blown to prevent us from interdicting the trail—providing those clowns in Washington get up the nerve to let us cross the border, that is.

"Instead of the usual one platoon on the road, one beating the bush, and one on reaction reserve, we've got two on the road, and one in the bush in the daytime and back here at night. As per usual, Somolik and 3d are in the bush. One of their tanks is down, so off you go Black. They'll be here this evening and you can link up with them then.

"Zumbro," he continued, "I know the dozer's a bit sick, but is there anything that would prevent you from sitting on a bridge for a while?"

"No sir. In fact, she won't even leak if all we're doing

155

is charging batteries. The leak is in the right-hand torque converter when a load is on it.''

''Good, we'll pair you with an infantry squad in one of those modified APCs; we've got a bridge that needs a permanent force until the LRRPs nail the local VC base force for us.''

''Okay sir, but what's the problem with this particular bridge?''

''All the other bridges can be bypassed by tanks with no problem, if they're blown,'' he said. ''But getting around this one would be a bitch, so they've earmarked it for special attention.''

I've always gotten on well with officers and, since we had some time to spare, he sat down and gave me the story.

''As I said, this one is critical. First, the VC blew the original French structure, and the engineers built a new one. The local command put a small garrison of Puffs on it, and forgot about it. A month later, a larger VC force came in, killed off the Puffs, and blew the bridge.''

''That's two so far,'' I cut in.

''And only half the story,'' he said, with a sardonic smile. ''The engineers constructed another bridge, and a permanent force of ARVN was stationed there. Then when Tet came, a main-force NVA company drove off the ARVN, losing half their number doing it, and blew the damn bridge again.''

''Christ!'' I exclaimed. ''Those people are serious.''

''But you haven't heard the last of it. We have a tank-laid bridge up at Battalion, and someone got the bright idea of having the AVLB [Armored Vehicle Laid Bridge] lay its bridge in the morning and take it home at night. That worked for a few weeks, but then Charlie blew the bridge tank with a command mine. Now there's a new engineer bridge, with permanent parking pads for two armored vehicles at each end of it; and, since you can't move too fast anyway, you're it.''

''Thanks for the background, Lieutenant. I'll give the crew the word and we'll get moving.''

''Don't hurry, Zippo. There's one tank on it already for tonight.''

I saluted and got out of there, thinking that we were due for a long, boring spell of guard duty.

Chapter Thirteen

LIFE AT A STRONGPOINT

With hands held over my head, alternately clenching and straightening, I gave Kennet the signals to direct the Executioner onto a parking pad on the west end of Bridge 15. There were four of these pads, two on each end of the bridge, and we set up on the northwestern one. Opposite us, on the other end of the bridge was the infantry track. In actuality, though, there was no squad of infantry—only a battalion recon vehicle and a few clerks detailed for "field duty."

A recon, or ACAV, is an M113 armored personnel carrier, with one .50 caliber MG, and a pair of .30s added. While it is a potent fighting machine, throwing half a dozen clerks and cooks into it does not create an instant infantry squad.

The 69th was always shorthanded, so we had to hold that critical bridge with whatever could be scraped up—

any warm body was fair game. Sometimes we had actual combat soldiers, and sometimes we were stuck with Headquarters specialists. Our preference, all too seldom granted, was Montagnard Puffs; they were natives and knew the territory. With a squad of these in residence, we could rest in confidence most of the time, assured that our perimeter was secure.

Checking around our new home, I could see why that bridge was so critical. It butted up against a steep ridge that ran north and south for many miles and, while a tank could eventually cross it without the bridge, a day would be lost in the process. With the bridge in place, forces from Pleiku could be at the Cambodian border in a few hours.

A few hundred feet to the south of us, the gaunt remains of the original French bridge lay barren and broken. I noticed in it a peculiar feature of VC bridge-wrecking technique. The abutments, or foundations of the bridge, had been left intact, and that indicated that the demo crew had had an ulterior motive. If a span is to be completely destroyed, the charges must be planted just behind the abutments; then the entire base of the bridge is blown, and it takes weeks of work to undo the damage. If only the actual roadway is destroyed, a new structure can be in place in a matter of hours.

Since this series of bridges was so close to the Cambode border, it looked as if the Cong, in leaving the abutments standing, were preparing the way for an invading army, rather than simply revolting against the existing government. This seems to be standard operating procedure for the communists. They trot out their usual dogma; then they slip in a couple of divisions while the news media are giving credence to the "peaceful revolutionaries."

Past the bridge structures, we could see the stair-stepped green of rice terraces climbing to meet the ridgeline. There were several hamlets in the picture-perfect distance, and we wondered which ones housed the Viet Cong.

The road itself was busy with the varied traffic of a tropical, rural community. Tiny schoolgirls, each with a brilliant, blue sun hat, passed us in the mornings and evenings. Each one carried a leather-bound textbook, and they would wave and invariably call out, "Hi, GI." Women of all ages passed by, balancing an incredible variety of cargo on the uniquely Asian shoulder sticks. A short-stepping, level gait is required to make this system work, and this stride makes it possible to spot a rural woman—even when she is dressed up and in the city. The city folk refer to the load yoke as "dummy sticks."

Men seemed to prefer to carry their loads in pairs, and we would see huge amounts of weight being hauled by two diminutive men with a pole across their shoulders. For the most part, the weight consisted of animals or produce, but we also saw small engines, firewood, and (once) a fifty-five-gallon drum half full of liquid being hauled this way.

Americans grow up thinking of a bicycle as either a sport vehicle or as transportation, but in Vietnam, the bike replaces the family sedan, station wagon, and pickup truck. It is not unusual to see a Vietnamese youth pedaling happily along, with his brand-new bride sitting demurely on the crossbar of his bicycle—their worldly goods behind them in bamboo baskets.

On market days, we would see a farmer coming down the road with chickens tied to the handlebars, a young pig strapped to the carrier, and a half-stalk of bananas slung under the seat. If the cargo was too heavy to pedal, the man pushed the bike, using it as a tandem-wheeled cart.

Buffalo-, cow-, or horse-drawn carts were the next step up in transportation, and normally only showed up on market days in the towns. Mechanization ran the gamut from A to B—motor scooters and Lambretta ditty wagons. Scooters appeared to be status symbols and were never overloaded. But those poor three-wheelers are the pickup trucks of Asia. They always had a full load of people, produce, lumber, whatever. They'd come wheezing down the road, and when a hill threatened to bring them to a halt, the people would all hop out, push it up the incline, then get back in and coast down the other side.

Of course, the fact that there was a lot of unspent cash lying around in our tanks and personnel carriers wasn't lost on the Vietnamese. We might as well have had dollar signs painted on our turrets. Capitalistic by nature, they quickly started competing for our business. The farmers stopped by to sell a portion of their produce for more than it would bring in the village. The ice merchants came by, trying to arrange an exclusive, bidding against each other for sole rights to service a given tank. Even our dirty laundry became a subject for these natural entrepreneurs. One girl got the laundry contract by agreeing to come to our bridge and do the washing there, so that we could get it back the same day.

Most of the trade was done with piasters, but we also used scrip and the barter system. Our C rations were hot barter items until we figured out why. Some of the LRRP people reported finding C rats on VC, and it didn't take long to figure out that VC sympathizers were converting perishable produce to canned food. After that, word went out throughout the country to stop the practice. One of the crews in 1st Platoon, down toward An Khe, had hosted a LRRP team, and someone got a bright idea. They swapped one last case of "Cs" to a farmer, followed him to his VC buddies, and let them get settled. Then they called in artillery. War is full of dirty tricks.

The villagers got in the habit of doing business with the GIs, and then trading with each other on the tank site.

Suddenly, we were a marketplace. At first, we didn't quite know how to take all the activity, but since the people were able to detect the VC, we used them as "Cong detectors." If no one showed up, we got nervous; and sure enough, there'd be some activity in the form of snipings, village shakedowns, or an ambush.

If kids were around, though, everything was safe; we could literally come out and play. The Viet and Montagnard children were an absolute riot. It wasn't at all unusual to see a bunch of them playing "hogpile" next to the ACAV, with a GI on the bottom, while a Puff trooper cleaned his MG and watched the crazy Americans. One of 3d Platoon's men, Simmons, the new gunner for A-Go-Go, sent home for a football, and we filled many boring afternoons playing tackle football with the kids—then afterwards we'd all go for a swim under the bridge.

Down in 1st Platoon's area, the situation was different, due to the presence of one of the few large VC units left. When the tanks had gone back to their road-guard jobs, several of the crews had taken up where they'd left off with their little Viet followings. The story came up to us about one gunner who had a bad encounter with a little boy.

When lots of kids are around, there is no problem, but one child alone is grounds for suspicion. The tanker was sitting on the turret cleaning a .45. He was handing the parts to his Vietnamese girlfriend who was putting the weapon back together. As soon as the woman put the recoil spring plug back, she slid a magazine in, racked the slide, and with absolutely no warning, shot a little boy who had been sidling up to the tank. As she and the shocked gunner dove behind the turret, the grenade that had been in the kid's hand blew up, killing him and peppering the tank.

Who killed that child—the woman, or the VC who sent him out, knowing that an eight-year-old couldn't possibly throw a frag far enough to be safe from the shrapnel? The label of "baby killer" should be put where it rightfully belongs—on the Viet Cong.

Up in 2d Platoon's zone, another boy ran up to Sergeant Ferguson on the 2-5 tank. Almost exhausted, he was screaming that the VC were in his village. The sergeant, unable to leave his section of the road, got on the radio, and was patched through to Division, who sent out a platoon of gunships and a company of infantry—catching Charlie with his pants down. That boy deserves a medal, because he saved his village from losing military-age males to the VC draft. (By the Cong's estimate, military age is from twelve years on up.)

The war took so many young men that, in our area, the only males of combat age were the Montagnard tribesmen and, at times, they were the only anti–Viet Cong forces around Pleiku.

Customarily, the Viets and the 'yards don't have much use for each other, preferring to go their separate ways. With the hill people fighting for them, though, the distinction got somewhat blurred. There were even a few marriages that thoroughly scandalized the neighborhoods. The Puffs operated as a militia, spending most of their time off duty, rotating spells of patrol or combat.

We never did figure their system out, unless the enlistment was for a whole family, as well as the head of a household. I could be sitting on the turret, watching the world go by, when a tribal male, dressed in a breechcloth and carrying a child in something that resembled a papoose carrier, would walk up and start talking with the Popular Forces squad leader. Then, one of the Puffs would walk up to the newcomer, and strip off his uniform. They would trade the kid for the carbine. The new man would put on the uniform, while the "relieved" man took the child and disappeared into the jungle. Weird.

Night was always the sticky time. The ARVN and the Puffs weren't night fighters, so the darkness belonged to the VC and the Americans. Having too few men to set up a defensive perimeter, we had to depend on technology and condensed nastiness to eliminate surprises. H&I fire was one of our favorite ways of keeping Charlie off balance, and there were several versions of this.

For close-in work, we preferred the M79 grenade gun, and we developed some good techniques for it. This weapon looks like a short, fat, single-barrel shotgun. Since the Cong learned to recognize its distinctive muzzle blast, they knew, once they heard it, that whoever was using it would be reloading and vulnerable to return fire. When you fired a grenade at a suspicious blur on a moonlit night, the enemy would wait for the sound of the grenade going off before standing up to shoot. However, by shooting at a sharp elevation, the projectile would be in the air long enough for you to reload. Then when it hit and exploded, the sniper would fire, revealing his position, and one more shot would nail him.

Since it was possible for a determined group of raiders to swim under the bridge and set charges, we got into the habit of periodically dropping grenades down into the darkness, just to keep any intruders on their toes. We also mounted several claymores on the underside of the bridge itself, aimed straight down—just in case. I rigged several trip flares in strategic locations, each one covered by a claymore; the detonators were laid in a row in front of the driver's hatch.

The tank itself was a fairly good anti-intrusion device, because the infrared searchlight could be on for a while without draining the battery. By using the searchlight on IR and scanning with the night sight, we nabbed quite a few "midnight skulkers." The driver had his own IR equipment, and we'd hang a couple of claymores on the dozer blade, just for safety's sake. We never caught anybody that way, but the capability gave us a feeling of comfort.

By using the turret's artillery controls we could pick out interesting spots during the day, range on them, record the data, and then fire at odd intervals during the night. There was a little instruction card for whoever was on watch, giving the elevation, deflection, and type of ammo to be used—as well as reminders not to forget to drop a grenade every so often. It's no wonder we were always so sleepy.

One night we received word to move out. The next day, as Somolik led his platoon towards us, our diesel was ticking over, and we were anticipating a spell in the bush. The vegetation close to the border varied from pastures and paddies to triple-canopy jungle, and it was necessary to adopt techniques for each kind of terrain. The lieutenant had long since become a master at this kind of "jungle-tanking," and I felt confident going into the hills with my old fraternity and its unconventional leader. The Apostle was laid up for transmission repairs, and we were to act as replacement, returning to the bridge at night.

This limitation would ordinarily have put something of a crimp in the platoon's free-ranging style, but intelligence was fairly sure that we were close to a large pocket of VC. So the plan was for short-range sweeps, trying to panic the enemy into doing something stupid. We kept at this for several days, using the infantry as "beaters," with the aim of driving the Cong into the guns of the 3d Platoon. Then for a few days, the process was reversed, giving the foot-sloggers a rest, while the diesels punched holes in the forest and brush.

We were in the kind of heavy, vine-festooned terrain that requires day after day of machete work for a mile or two of walking. But the tanks were taking it in stride, ripping the foliage and dropping trees to make room for the hulls. Some of the trees were too large to push over, but these were far enough apart to drive between. Anything less than two feet in diameter could be dropped with some strain, and the smaller stuff was not worth mentioning.

There were two exceptions, though. One was the ironwood tree, with wood so dense that it won't float and a taproot so deep that a six-inch specimen would stop a dozer-tank cold. We soon learned to recognize the pale, greyish bark and to drive around it. The other exception was a short, inoffensive-looking large-leaved tree that had a huge root system. When one of these was pushed out of the way, it would pivot at ground level and the root crown would come up under the hull, lifting you clear of contact with terra firma, leaving the tracks churning helplessly a few inches from the ground. It took only one experience of this to burn the tree's leaf pattern into memory, because whoever pulled us off could charge the crew a case of beer, plus give the inevitable good-natured razzing.

The "lurps" (LRRPs) spotted signs of jungle-camp activity, and Command estimated that we were very close to flushing that hard-to-find pocket of resistance. On one particular day, the sweep pattern was changed just enough to throw that cagey bunch of bandits off balance. The plan was for the heavy section—Somolik and two other tanks, with a platoon of infantry riding the hulls—to make a halfhearted sweep through the target zone, and then lie doggo for a few hours while a company of ground troops marched overland to join them. Once they were in place, the light section of Ape and Executioner, along with two more platoons of grunts, would move straight toward the suspected base, attempting to drive Charlie into a trap.

We heard light small-arms fire over the ridge, and I told the squad leader, "Better drop your men to ground, Sarge;

it could blow up any second now." Acknowledging with a nod, he hand-signaled to his boys and they left the fenders, some leaping to the jungle floor, others sliding down convenient vines. The Ape's tank commander, Somolik's platoon sergeant, gave me a hand signal that brought me parallel with him, and we eased forward, drivers and loaders buttoned up, only the tank commander's hatches open. This is how you get it, I thought, a rocket in the chest and ride home in a rubber bag.

Third Platoon and the infantry company were really close now. The bark of M16s was mixed with the deeper sound of AK47s and the yammer of Soviet-made Degtyarev machine guns. No battle plan survives contact with the enemy, and this was no exception. We were a bit off in our locations and, instead of driving the VC towards Somolik and that reinforced company, the enemy was being driven towards us! The trap was working but it was inside out; the anvil was falling on the hammer.

Precious little sunlight manages to get all the way down to the forest floor, but I could see black-clad shapes flitting towards us; Sanchez was holding the sights on a group of them. Unbelievably, the sound of the heavy section masked our arrival and, when Ape, Executioner, and our infantry cut loose, they were caught by surprise. We had no preconceived plan or firing signal, but experienced combat men know when to open up for maximum effect.

We spread the two tanks apart just far enough to allow some VC to get between us so we could put them in a crossfire; then each of us became a fire-breathing armored fort, deep in a gloomy, green, fire-punctuated jungle. The Cong evidently thought that our two machines were part of a larger force, and they concentrated on us, trying to break through a nonexistent line, while three more tanks and a reinforced company steadily closed in on them.

A fire-spitting crash caught my eye, and as I turned to

the right rear, the hull shuddered and flames leaped from the engine grilles. In order to see the extent of the damage, I had to swing the turret to the right, which put me in a position peering straight down into an inferno. A rocket team had shot from close concealment putting one into our belly, setting the fuel tanks on fire. Dark red-orange fire was licking along both sides of the back deck and oily black smoke was rolling skyward toward the green canopy.

Thank God for diesel engines. If the old girl had been a gasoline fueled tank, we would be dead.

"Kennet, we are on fire—do not panic—pull number one extinguisher—now." In a predicament like this the commander's voice is the crew's only link with sanity, and it's imperative to remain calm.

I switched to platoon commo and sent out a call: "All Chopper three elements, this is niner; I am on fire and cannot fight." At that moment, the built-in CO_2 extinguisher went off and the flames subsided as if by magic.

"Hit the starter, Kennet, and let's get going again." With a thud and a whine the starter went in, the engine caught, but the flames also caught once more, leaping high enough to singe my arms. "Goddammit! Extinguisher again." Kennet released the second and last charge of the built-in system, and the flames died again.

Now this *is* a pretty pickle, I thought; every time the starter throws a spark, we catch on fire. The situation was getting difficult. The VC knew they had a cripple, and were still under the impression they had to break out. Sanchez was in the turret reporting more and more of them and steadily working the co-ax, when suddenly the clearing was filled with thundering, flaming, olive-drab dinosaurs.

With a heaving, roaring crash, the platoon was around us and the tanks were slamming trees to the ground in a long-practiced method creating an instant fort for the riflemen. They came in a line, each picking a green column, smashing it to earth, and then taking up a protected position in the hole where the roots had been. Soldiers then lined up along the trunk or found safe places in the crown and began to dig in.

By this time I had my crew out, and was racking my brain for a way out of this mess. The engine could start and run, but the fuel leaking from the belly blow would catch fire, and the extinguishers would then suffocate the engine.

"Kennet, get me the tool bag." Dropping to the ground, I took the wrench he handed me and loosened the maintenance access plates under the hull and drained some of the collected fuel. Meanwhile, Sanchez and Kennet opened the engine grilles.

"Try water cans this time," I said, "and let's see if we can float the fire out." With our crew and the men from other tanks standing tensely on the engine deck, all holding water cans and portable extinguishers, I dropped into the driver's seat and hit the starter.

"We're burning again!" Sanchez hollered over the intercom. He was standing on the turret, right over the fuel tanks, supervising the fire detail.

"All right, Sanchez, start 'em pouring."

"Right, Sarge." Then after a moment he shouted, "It worked, Zippo! The fire is washing out the access ports."

Heaving a sigh of relief, I keyed the helmet to radio and got hold of Somolik. "Three-six, this is Niner."

"Yeah, I see your problem, Zippo; good job. If I give you an escort to the road, can you make it back to company base?"

"Roger; as soon as they've closed the grille doors, we can move." Leaving Sanchez in the tank commander's position, I decided to drive out myself, keeping a close eye on the temperature gauges. There was no telling what else had been fried by the fire. With the Ape tagging along, babysitting the cripple, we followed our own tread marks back out and were soon on the road.

I was back in the tank commander's hatch, and we were rolling towards company base, when the captain got on the radio net: "Chopper Niner, this is Chopper 6, can you still operate your turret?"

"Roger, but if I shut down and have to start up again, we'll have another fire."

"I know, goddammit, but I've got two more cripples that can't move at all. You have to sit on that bridge to-night; it has to be held at all costs." We had a heated discussion over the radio, but a buck sergeant can't out-argue a company commander; so we pulled into the same pad at Bridge 15, and I made plans to ensure our survival.

Reading between the lines, we knew that Captain Biggio had something going that was more important than one crippled tank and its crew, so we were almost on our own. After refilling our water cans from the stream, we opened the armored grille door, collected all the fire extinguishers that had been given to us by the platoon, and prepared to blast off if things got too hot to handle.

We covered all bets by rigging our explosives in among the 90mm H.E. shells, so that if we couldn't start and run, we could blow the old girl and hitch a ride with the ACAV. Fortunately, the Cong were preoccupied; there was a hell of a ruckus going on out in the woods—we could still hear the nineties. We kept our radios on platoon frequency, so we could follow the action. It wasn't a big fight; it was just that our personal part in it had become a little too hot.

After one very spooky night, 3d Platoon broke out of night laager and, dropping off a replacement at the bridge, they escorted us in. We cranked the diesel and, after putting out the fire, tucked in next to last in line.

"Niner, this is Assassin. Your left track is wobbling."

Turning to look back, I could see the drive sprocket wandering around on its hub. After pulling over, our fears were comfirmed—the drive bolts, one by one, were fatiguing and snapping.

By reducing speed to five miles per hour, we arrived at the company firebase, and limped up to the maintenance tent. The Executioner was leaking transmission oil and leaving a trail of smoke everywhere we went. At least one track was about to fall off, and a hole was burned in the armor. To add insult to injury, the roadwheel hubs were overheating and the batteries were going bad. The dozer-blade hydraulics had long since died, and two more torsion bars were gone. The Executioner was in mortal danger of fatal collapse.

"Look at it this way," the ordnance tech said. "There's thirteen thousand miles on this self-propelled disaster, and they're supposed to be turned in for complete rebuild at five thousand. You haven't been running this tank, you've been coaxing it along on willpower."

"Well how long will it take to get another one up here from Qui Nhon?"

"You're outta luck, Sarge; there ain't another one of these dozers in-country—maybe not in the Pacific Command. We're gonna have to order one from the States."

"Christ," Sanchez said, "that'll take weeks, and I don't want to hang around base camp doing infantry patrol. What're we gonna do, Zippo?"

"Well, fellas," I announced, "it's about time for a little R&R, so the old sarge is going to Bangkok. See ya in a week."

Chapter Fourteen

BUSH-BEATING AT FIREBASE SCHUELLER

Bangkok, Thailand, was, for me, the ideal place for rest and recuperation. That country is the only Indochinese nation that was never colonized, and its people are more like Americans than any other Asian nation. Their women have been liberated for a hundred years, and there's no social stigma on prostitution. Many Thais speak English as a second language, so communication was a breeze. Their beer is magnificent—they'd imported German brewmasters, malt, and hops, and the resultant ambrosia cost only one baht (26¢) a liter.

For what more could a tired GI ask? I slept for thirty hours, ate enormous amounts of good food, and went shopping. The girls were pretty and the beer plentiful. This ol' sergeant consumed more of both than was good for him, and returned to A Company refreshed and renewed, but with every intention of making another trip to the "Venice of the East."

They'd moved again! If you turned your back on Company A for one week, they were gone. When I got back in-country and returned to Camp Enari, the staff sergeant who ran our rear area detachment clued me in.

"Second Platoon had to go up to the Special Forces base at Plei Mei, and counter an NVA raid on the camp, and they're still up there looking for trouble. But 3d, 1st, and Company Headquarters have moved down to that old Firebase Schueller, between An Khe City and Mang Yang Pass. And when 2d gets down there, it's bush-beating time again."

"Well goddamn," I said. "That's mostly up and down terrain, with jungles growing out of the sides of mountains."

"Don't ask me why. I'm just an E6, and that's where the brass wants us. There's NVA in there someplace, cause the truckers have been catching hell all over that whole damned roller-coaster section. Oh yeah, one more bit of news. Yer buddy, Lieutenant Joe, ain't with us anymore; he's been shipped to Headquarters Company for his six months of staff duty. Third's got a new boss, Lieutenant Daniels."

That, I thought, would not appeal to Somolik, but it was policy that all officers had to spend half of their tour in combat and half on staff duty, to round out their experience. So now 3d's fire-eating skipper would be tied to a desk. (I should have known better. He was out in the hills in less than a month.)

"Well, how do I get to company base, by land or chopper?"

"There's a five-tonner loaded with a new set of tracks

for three of 1st Platoon's tanks. It's up at Battalion motor pool now, and you're to ride shotgun with him.''

"Great, do we tag onto a convoy, or do we have an escort?''

"You're okay out through Pleiku City," he said, "and down that long highland strip as far as the top of the pass; there's always a tank there, waiting to escort convoys or stragglers through the rough section.''

"Fine, just gimme a half hour to get these Class A's stashed and pick up something that shoots, and I'll be right along.''

We were nearly ready to pull out of the motor pool, when the personnel sergeant came over and snagged my driver. "Sorry about this, Sarge," he said to me. Then he turned to my driver, "Jackson, your rotation came through. You're to begin processing out.''

I couldn't ask a man in that position to make one last run, so I asked the Battalion motor sergeant, who had wandered over, for another driver.

"No can do Sarge," he said, "till I get some warm bodies back from Qui Nhon. Most of my wheelers are down on the coast picking up supplies, and that was my last driver.''

"Yeah, I can see your problem, but the company's gotta have these tracks ASAP.''

He looked at me in a speculative manner and said, "You're the one they call Zippo, aren't you?''

"Sure, but what's that got to do with it?''

"Well, you've got a rep for getting results and keeping quiet, and you got one of my men, Gray, promoted with that two-page recommendation you sent in. So I figure I owe you some cooperation.'' By then, the staff clerk had wandered off and we were alone.

"Tell you what," he said. "You can take the truck yourself and wait for the evening escort at the junction. I'll ride you past the gate, so the MPs don't ask any questions, and you can drop me off at that Vietnamese welding shop.''

By now my brain was fully back in the war, and working fast. He obviously didn't know that the company had moved its headquarters way down the road, or he never would have worked out that plan. Apparently, he thought we were still at the base out on Highway 19 West, just a few hours from Enari.

''Sure thing,'' I said. ''Let's roll.'' After dropping him off at whatever unofficial business he had going, I turned off the road and drove under a shade tree. I'd never driven a five-tonner before, so I took out the truck's manual and made sure there were no mechanical snags waiting for me. Once I'd memorized the shift pattern, mastered that tricky transfer case, and checked out the ring-mounted Browning, I headed down 19E bound for An Khe—racing the sun to meet the escort tank at the top of the pass.

The outfit was in an already-established firebase, sharing a cramped perimeter with a battery of light 105 towed howitzers, a few infantry, a section of LRRPs, a platoon of MPs, and an engineer squad. It was a real hodgepodge.

''Welcome back, Sarge,'' Kennet said, as I parked the five-tonner. ''Where's your driver?''

''Don't have one. I came solo and tagged onto the sunset run, following the Assassin home. Where's maintenance set up?''

''Over there behind the mess tent,'' he pointed. ''They don't have a setup yet. They're working out of the shop truck and the VTR.'' No one was around, so I left the truck and walked off, leaving the problem of its driver to someone else.

Without a tank, and stuck in company base, I knew what was going to happen without having to ask.

"That's right," Lieutenant Walker said. "We need your experience in supply and ammo shuffling till we get settled in here. Anyway, it will be a month or so until your new dozer tank arrives. And you wouldn't want to get bored, would you?"

For the next couple of weeks, it was business as usual—with a few added attractions. The ground was a compact of flint mixed with clay, a substance so hard that shovel tips bent and pickaxes bounced. The original bunkers had had their holes blasted into the ground before the troops moved in, but now the perimeter was too densely inhabited for heavy blasting. By driving a tanker's bar (six-foot wrecking bar) in with a sledge, we could make a small, deep hole. Then, working carefully, I would set fist-sized charges of TNT to break loose bushel-sized chunks of clay, until the surface layer had been removed and normal digging could resume.

In addition to the minidemo work inside the perimeter, we had to help set up the strong points along the portion of Highway 19E from An Khe to Mang Yang Pass. That part of the road is the critical link in the supply chain from the coastal port at Qui Nhon to the highlands, and it has seen many bloodbaths. The French lost an armored unit there in '54, and the rusted hulk of a Japanese tank stands as a sentinel over some long-forgotten catastrophe.

The open, rolling terrain of the highlands and the utterly flat coastal plain were both fairly safe, but the steep, twisting slopes in the central thirty miles invited ambush and attack. Constant terrain sweeps were conducted by infantry from the 173d Airborne and the 1st and 26th regiments of the Korean Capital Division. Company A was based out of LZ Schueller, providing point security and reaction capability in case of attack.

Stretched to the limit, we were supporting infantry patrols as well as guarding the highway. In addition, we were responsible for the defense of Schueller, roughly four acres of mixed units and highly vulnerable supplies and munitions. The LZ sat on an open knoll, surrounded by bare fields that sloped away from its defenses on three sides. The contested road passed our northern boundary, and beyond this was a level field that dropped off sharply into a deep ravine about three hundred yards north of the perimeter.

Our main defense was, as usual, double-apron barbed wire topped by a triple row of concertina. Buried in the entanglement was a mix of claymores, trip flares, and antipersonnel mines. Bunkers were spotted around the wire and the controls of the claymores led to these. Schueller could be sniped at from long range, but an actual assault would have been very costly.

The strong points were another matter. Each was exposed to enemy fire, and we were forced to defend the bridges to keep them from being blown at night. This put the troops in some sticky situations. First Platoon, under Lieutenant Wilson, drew the assignment of securing the bridges. Most of the time, they were secured by a reinforced squad of paratroopers, and the tanks were concentrated where the danger was greatest. But we had three of these miniature forts to protect, and five tanks with which to accomplish the mission.

The posts were known as check points (CPs). The one nearest the LZ was easiest, because it was located on level ground and could easily be rescued by a column from Schueller. The other two were farther away and in a far worse situation. They were dominated by towering, green-jungled mountains, some as high as five thousand feet. They provided excellent cover for the NVA, and allowed them concealed access both to the two bridges and to the stretch of blacktop between them. This section of road was so exposed that the truckers called it "Ambush Alley."

These mountains were full of caves and were within sniper and mortar range of the convoy route. The drivers were shot at, mortared, and mined daily. The CPs themselves were under almost constant night harassment until the tanks moved in.

As the company developed its plans, the ammo and fuel section was put to work, and it was fortunate that they now included an experienced tank crew, one that knew the needs of the combat units. Since night H&I fire was standard procedure, I was kept constantly moving, supplying the CPs with 90mm, co-ax, ammo, 40mm, and claymores. The crews had built bunkers and beefed up the defenses with sandbag parapets and fifty-five-gallon drums full of sand.

To reduce the snipings and eliminate concealment for ambushes, the tankers and engineers adopted a policy of clearing a wide strip on both sides of the road, and around each check point. This was accomplished by a combination of dozing and burning, and it kept me busy, hauling gasoline for the brush burns, as well as ammo for the tanks. Running without escort most of the time, we were targets for snipers, and we picked up the habit of changing speed and taking sudden cross-country shortcuts.

Since the tanks were supporting close-in infantry patrols with gunfire, and keeping an eye on the road, we had to take the supplies to them rather than be met at the road. This led to some hair-raising incidents. One time, Sergeant Taylor, who was beating up a mortar position for a squad of paratroopers, radioed in for more H.E.P., and, intending to top off his entire platoon while we were at it, Rich and I took out the five-tonner. When we got within sight of them, there were only two passable routes to the ridge from which he was firing. One route led along the ridge itself, which would leave us skylined, and the other led across a freshly burned, still-smoldering field.

Not wanting to expose our sensitive explosives to hostile fire, we drove over the field, using the heavy smoke for cover, dodging some still-burning brush piles. Taylor, appalled at the risk, but agreeing with the choice, had us wait until his fire mission was over; he then shepherded us along the ridge, keeping his tank's bulk between us and any possible snipers. Episodes like that were commonplace and, looking back, I'd guess that Rich and I must have worn most of the feathers off of our guardian angels.

With one platoon on CP duty, one kept as a reaction force, and one spread out with the infantry manning a couple of daytime strong points, our forces were strained. Sometimes the reserve was on convoy escort, as well as being available for combat action. Even the tank retriever was pressed into service, protecting LZ Schueller's motley collection of supply vehicles on their weekly run to An Khe. The retriever had only a single .50 Browning, but they would load it with cooks and clerks armed with submachine guns and make like a tank. The one time they were jumped, the motor sergeant, an E7 named Mitten, leaned out of the hatch and, firing a 66mm LAW one-handed, shot an RPG gunner who was drawing a bead on the VTR. Both warheads went off and the NVA was vaporized.

The company was nearly stretched to the limit again when Lieutenant Somolik pulled a fast one and got back to the field. Following the policy of assigning officers to six months in base and six months in combat, Joe Somolik had been assigned to Headquarters Company. But when the lieutenant who ran the Battalion recon platoon became a casualty, Joe volunteered to fill the slot. Not only did that assignment cover his "Headquarters requirement," but it got the combat-hungry officer back where he was happiest—and solved our biggest problem at the same time.

Our worst hassle was filling our need for light, fast,

combat vehicles, as well as the heavy murder machines. A traditional armored-cavalry troop has a mix of ACAVs and heavy tanks, allowing the troop to fill a variety of roles. Company A was a heavy-assault unit, with battle tanks designed for another kind of war; now we needed to acquire a "light-maneuver" element.

By an odd coincidence, the Battalion mortar platoon was wandering around loose. Because of the excellence of our artillery coverage, the mortars weren't needed and they couldn't replace the tubes, which they'd worn out months before. Those mortars were 4.2 inch, heavy models, mounted in modified M113 tracked carriers—the same vehicle used by the recon platoon. With a little A Company–style maneuvering, Somolik got those six mortar tracks temporarily assigned to the recon section. He scrounged up some ACAV conversion kits for them, and was assigned to back up Captain Biggio on the pass. Lieutenant Joe had left the company only a month before, headed for an administrative job, and now he was back with fourteen ACAVs that he'd damn near conjured up out of thin air.

Those tracks gave us a capability we hadn't had before. They could go places that would bog or stall a tank—if necessary, they could "swim," using the tracks as paddle wheels.

We were able to maneuver fairly well in this mountainous, overgrown terrain, providing we observed certain rules. The most important was not to tackle the steep slopes with tanks. Here, the heavy vehicles either ran the bottoms or the ridgelines, traversing the distance between the two by following natural grades or passes. Instead of using our "belly-to-belly" tactics, the tanks were now shooting from one slope to another, their guns directed by radio from ACAVs or infantry squads. The guns were now being used to hit targets three and four thousand yards away, along with our regular short-range work.

Of course, with all this search and destroy activity going on, the ammo-supply section stayed busy. Oddly enough, one of the hardest items to keep in supply was the 40mm round for the grenade guns. There was actually a quota on them, and since the extra tracks weren't official, I had to sneak the munitions past red tape to keep my boys supplied.

There was also a continuous demand for flares and incendiaries, since part of the job was burning abandoned habitations to deny the NVA use of them; the local populace had been consolidated into fortified villages. The captain believed that this operation was taking too much time, and wanted to speed things up. One day, he called me over to his jeep, which had a tarpaulin-covered trailer hitched to it.

Throwing back the tarp, he said to me, "Here's 90 percent of a flamethrower and the tech manual. Think you can make it work?" Giving it a quick once-over, I could see that more than 10 percent was missing, but it didn't appear hopeless.

"Yes sir, but I'll have to liberate some parts. That thing is an engineer item, but we can probably get the parts from the paratroopers down at An Khe base."

"Well, that's why it's hooked up to my jeep," he said. "Take my driver and get what you need."

It took the better part of a week to get the engine for the charging compressor, and to find the fittings to connect the flame nozzle to the pressure hose. We finally were able to get the trigger matches from supply, and the weapon was complete.

A flamethrower can burn a variety of fuels, from gasoline to napalm, depending upon the job at hand. Not wanting to go through the mess of making napalm, we decided on a mixture of military gasoline and crankcase oil from the tanks—with a small amount of axle grease stirred in for "body."

When the diabolical machine was charged and filled, we went outside the perimeter wire for test firing. The captain, not sure of the recoil of all that pressure, braced himself against my back and, the exec standing by with a camera, I let go. The first match fizzled, but the second caught, and then the fire mix came out in a fine, swirling, red ball. We'd got the concoction just right the first time— all we needed was positive hootch ignition, not the reach of gelled fuel. With that, the company had acquired another capability. From then on, one of my men was kept busy, loading the flamegun and nursing a somewhat flaky compressor.

Several days later, I was out with 2d Platoon, which had drawn patrol duty. My flamethrower and a few cases of explosives were strapped to the sides of the 2-5 tank, the Apache. Its boss, Sergeant Ferguson, a muscular, brown-haired man, was filling me in on his outfit's adventures as we climbed a forested hillside.

"Right after you left for Thailand, the word came down that North Viet armor had been spotted coming down the Ho Chi Minh Trail, and the Old Man ordered that each tank be issued HEAT [high-explosive antitank] shells, in case we got a crack at the enemy tanks. Remember how many tanks were supposedly 'broken down' and sitting in company base?" he asked.

"Yeah, seems like each platoon had one or two pulling that stunt to get a break in the monotony."

"I'll tell ya, when the chance to tackle some honest-to-God enemy armor showed up, all hidden spare parts came out of wherever they were hidden and, before the ammo truck got back to Pleiku, every tank in the company reported in, ready and running. Damnedest thing I ever saw.

Third Platoon was still recuperating from that mess you got shot up in, so when the Green Beanie boys up at Plei Mei called for help, Sergeant 'T' called out 'saddle up,' and we took off for the border."

The North Viets had apparently decided to take a page out of our book of tricks, and use tanks to bust a particularly bothersome base. The Plei Mei Special Forces camp had been a thorn in their sides for some months. The Popular Forces and a few ARVN units operating out of it had slowed traffic on the Trail considerably. One morning, the Green Berets heard engines and tracks in the jungle, and anxiously radioed in to 4th Division, asking if they had any tanks in the area, hoping the noise came from them. When Division Headquarters radioed back in the negative, the Special Forces CO said: "Well, if you haven't got any here now, we're gonna need some, ASAP."

Shortly after that, a dozen PT76s roared out of the jungle, running off the infantry and shooting the camp to ribbons. The SFs had "gone to ground" in their deepest bunker, and that's where 2d found them. When their outposts spotted the tiger-faced M48s coming up the trail, the amphibious Russian-built tanks simply bugged out.

"Lieutenant Walker had the fastest tank and the best driver," Ferguson told me, "and he almost caught one, but they were across a stream and out of range before the rest of us got there. Damned incompetent bunch of people, too; they couldn't bust infantry out of bunkers, and the SF bunkers aren't even as strong as the ones the VC build down in the plains."

"Did you ever get another crack at them?" I asked, as Apache ground to a halt in a deserted village.

"Nope, never saw or heard them again. But maybe they'll try some other time; I always wanted to take on another tank head-to-head."

* * *

We had an engineer with a mine detector along with us, as well as two squads of infantry riding on the tanks, and as the tanks fanned out, each covering a segment of a perimeter, we dismounted and went to work. The riflemen formed into groups and carefully probed for resident hostiles, while the detector operator swept the hootches and the entire area for hidden supplies. Sometimes, we'd find a food stash, or an arms cache, but this place was abandoned to rats and roaches.

"Okay Zippo," Sergeant Taylor called out. "Your turn."

Prior to getting the flamethrower, the task of torching one of these settlements was tedious. The troops had had to set fires individually, or use 37mm flares modified to fit the M79s. Now, as the infantry mounted up on the other two vehicles, I merely stood on Apache's back deck and loosed two fireballs, one to each side of the compound. Then we lined up, ready for the next objective.

Chapter Fifteen

AMBUSH AT AN KHE PASS

Rumors were flying about NVA reinforcements in the An Khe area, and the pass had become ominously quiet. Our intelligence, usually of little or no value where communist plans were concerned, suddenly became deadly accurate. It was so accurate that one sergeant described it this way: "If intelligence says that an NVA colonel is gonna shit in the middle of the pass, drop off a roll of paper on your way through, because he'll be there." If the info was that good, we thought, why not jump their base camp and nail the whole bunch?

The reason is that American minds, especially the military versions, are a lot more devious than most folks would admit. Why should we go into their jungle? the brass reasoned. Let them come out to our road, and they can dance to our music.

Years after being in Vietnam, I heard that the South

Vietnamese had had a corps of women who had volunteered to go into NVA and Cong camps as camp followers, and become mistresses of the enemy commanders. Someone like that must have been the source of much of our information. But not only did we know the approximate plans of the local enemy commander, we had also been informed of a new NVA regiment moving into our area. This last piece of intelligence was the result of a radio intercept by our old CO, Captain Allen, who was now Battalion S-2 (military intelligence).

The fuel for our machinery was brought up the road in five-thousand-gallon tanker trucks interspersed in the regular convoys. On this occasion, though, the word went out that a huge convoy of nothing but fuel trucks was coming up the pass. The North Viets had spies, too, and they were apparently allowed to find out about this convoy. We all knew about the continual spying, but details don't filter down to noncom levels that early in an operation. The first word I got that anything unusual was up, was when Richardson and I took the truck to An Khe base for a normal run, anticipating another boring day.

We were sitting in the truck cab, behind the firebase entrance, smoking and finishing our coffee. Waiting for the road to be opened for traffic, we began to notice changes from the usual routine. The daily procedure was first to scan the road, and the fields beside it, for signs of overnight activity, then to send out an MP/engineer team to check for mines. The "first light" scan was ordinarily done by helicopter, but this day, instead of an unarmed slick, the run was being made by a pair of gunships. Somebody was worried.

The section from LZ Schueller to An Khe was all that I was concerned with, though, and as soon as the MP "roadrunner" pulled up to the gate, I told Richardson to move out and I eased up into the ringmount.

"Hey, look Sarge, it's Company," he said, pointing to an incoming chopper. I had developed the habit of keeping a pair of 8×15 miniature binoculars in a shirt pocket; a quick check with these revealed the Battalion honcho, Colonel Riggs, seated in the Huey.

Something was up, all right. You get conscious of details in a combat zone; as the truck lurched into motion, we observed that the wood cutters going out for the day's work didn't have their kids with them, and that the Coca-Cola girls were late. No children, plus no girls, added up to a strong indication that the reinforced NVA units were going to try something—and soon—so we were very alert as we rolled along.

In most areas, the road had been cleared on both sides by engineer teams with Rome plows, and the brush was stripped back to one hundred fifty meters. The plows had dozed the uprooted vegetation into long rows perpendicular to the highway and, while the risk of ambush was greatly reduced, these rows could still harbor bad news so it was a relief to get into town. As we drove into An Khe base, we saw a seemingly endless line of five-thousand-gallon tankers, waiting for clearance to travel.

"That explains the precautions," I said to Rich. "They just don't want those fuel trucks blown."

One of the platoons had ordered demo supplies, so we picked up a quarter ton of C4 and TNT. We were just pulling into the ammunition section of the dump when one of our company trucks screeched to a halt alongside us, having broken the base speed limit by double.

"Hey, Zippo!" Sanchez yelled. "The 3d Platoon's smack in the middle of an ambush ten klicks past company base, and you're needed pronto!"

"All right, you take that truck and load 300 rounds of 90mm, half H.E. and half cannister; 100,000 rounds of 7.62 belted, with tracers; and 5,000 rounds of .50 caliber—and a couple cases of mixed grenades for each tank. Head for company base and wait for orders.''

We were in third gear by the time we hit the ammo-dump entrance and the main gate MP must have gotten the word, because he had stopped all traffic and waved us through. We took the righthand turn through the town on three wheels, terrorizing the civilians by running up the main drag wide open with the horn blaring, and the ring-mounted .50 punctuating the racket with a few bursts into the air.

Long before, the truck's governor had had a few shims put behind its speeder spring, and we got to the first bridge in record time. The MP there, a sergeant with a gun jeep, had traffic backed up for about two hundred yards, but I told Richardson to run up the shoulder to the bridge.

"Hold it up, Sarge," the MP said. "There's tanks and paratroopers in an ambush up in the pass, and all traffic is stopped for the duration."

"I know. That's our 3d Platoon," I said, pointing at our bumper ID for emphasis. "They're calling for resup-ply, and we've got their ammo. Now get that jeep out of the way, we've got a job to do."

Backing the vehicle out of the road, he looked up at us incredulously. "You're goin' in there with a load of H.E.?"

"Right, and there'll be another truck along in about forty-five minutes."

"You're nuts!" he yelled as we swept by, but he popped us a salute of respect as the truck picked up speed. The road was completely clear of traffic, and Richardson was able to use both sides of it, shortcutting the curves and keeping his speed up to the maximum.

We slammed to a halt outside the firebase entrance, and I told Richardson to keep the engine running while I went in for instructions. Captain Biggio quickly brought me up to date: "The roadrunner crew found a 105 shell about five klicks west of here and the EOD team went out to defuse it. The round was rigged for command detonation, and it was set off in the team's face. There had apparently been an ambush set for the fuel convoy, but the idiots jumped the road-clearing detail instead. Third Platoon and the scouts were already warming up for the day, anyway, so we sent them in. They're in the kill zone now, eating it up from the inside."

At that moment, the command radio broke in: "Chopper 6, this is 3-6, how are you coming on that resupply? We are low on cannister and H.E., and the swampy area has us blocked. The scouts are across it and infantry is airlifting in behind the ACAVs. The NVA have retreated to their staging point, and we are acting as direct-fire artillery. The gunships are orbiting, but if they run out of fuel and we run out of ammo at the same time, the infantry will be in a tight spot."

"Roger that," the Old Man answered. "Zippo is here with a full basic load, including grenades and demo." He released the mike switch and asked me, "Can you handle the scouts and a company of infantry too?"

Inventorying the truckload from memory, I replied, "Yes sir, but that'll completely strip out the 5.56."

"Chance we'll have to take," he said, keying the mike to call Lieutenant Daniels and the paratrooper CO.

The exec came in and told me, "I'm going out now, so we'll travel together for security. Have your driver follow my jeep." Giving the captain a fast salute, I went outside and spotted Cheyenne, whose tank was disabled with engine problems.

"Do you need any help, Zippo?" he asked.

"No, two of us are enough to handle the truck and the .50, and there'll be plenty of warm bodies at the other end to handle the unloading. Thanks anyway."

"Well don't do anything stupid. I'd hate to have to break in a new running mate."

"Okay," I said, running for the truck. "Roll it Rich, we're goin' in."

Arriving at the ambush site, we saw a spectacle of pure, bloody chaos. There were parts of dismembered humans scattered all over hell's half acre . . . literally. There were bodies on the road, in the bushes, and on top of the brush rows, where they'd been blown after being swept off a turret by a blast of cannister or co-ax from another tank. The ground had been churned to a mess by the tank tracks. And, here and there, you could see an arm or a leg mashed into part of a pushed-over tree.

Just around the bend, the MPs, engineers, and the remains of the EOD team, along with two infantry squads, had set up a nervous perimeter around the MP gun truck—a six-by with a motorized quad-fifty mount. They were guarding a landing zone for medevac.

The lieutenant dropped me off and went up the hill—very carefully—to check things out, since we could still hear the rattle of AKs and Degtyarevs. Leaving Richardson on the .50, I went over to the MP sergeant in the gun truck to find out what the hell had happened.

He told me. The ordnance man was about five feet from the 105 shell when the NVA set it off by remote control, killing him and badly wounding his crew. He was almost shredded and the other three were full of shrapnel and bleeding heavily. The MPs and engineers grabbed the wounded men to see what they could do for them, and got on the horn for medevac.

Just as they got the bleeding stopped, heavy small-arms fire began coming from a rising slope north of the hill.

"Contact!" the MP shouted. "We're taking heavy small-arms fire." They loaded the wounded onto the six-by and, with the quad mount raking the slope, they backed around the bend—out of the kill zone.

At this point, our CO was already on the way; as his unarmed slick whizzed low over the NVA position, it drew a stream of tracers. Trailing smoke and weaving, the chopper slanted off toward the road, the pilot trying desperately to avoid landing in enemy territory. With both door guns stitching the slope, aided by the MPs' quad mount, the ship bounced to a rough landing near the truck.

By now, the Battalion CO was on the scene in another bird; and, escorted by two gunships, the colonel had his chopper set down by the crippled one. They unloaded one wounded man, the artillery top sergeant, while the pilot and crew repaired the damage. It was just instrument damage, so the crew chief wired past it, making the ship airworthy again.

Incoming fire was still heavy, so the two Huey rocket-artillery choppers opened up on the hill, covering for the two unarmed ships, as they lifted out.

"At the moment they all got clear of the ground," the MP told me, "your lead tanks came around the bend like old-time cavalry. It was beautiful."

At LZ Schueller, 3d Platoon had been ready to go out to its assigned mobile strong points. Second had been topped off and was preparing for convoy escort, minus the 2-3 tank, which had its engine out, the crew looking for a fuel leak. The Scout platoon, also minus a few cripples, was going to "beat the bushes" and man several strong points.

When word of the contact came in, both our CO and the Battalion CO took to the air, and the combat vehicles that were ready simply cranked up and charged out at high speed, heading west toward the sound of firing. Sergeant Waller, the boss of the 2-3, had frantically thrown his tank back together and rushed off after his platoon, his crew still bolting the armored deck in place.

They knocked themselves into a formation, the Scouts tucking in between the tanks, as they covered the few kilometers to the ambush. And when they rumbled into the kill zone, seventeen armored monsters shot a well-laid ambush into doll rags.

Third Platoon was in the lead; the Ape, Assassin, A-Go-Go, Avenger, and the Apostle turned off the road in line abreast, along with the tanks of 2d and the Scout tracks. The lighter machines were spaced in among the heavies, but they hung back slightly as the "big boys" broke the back of the ambush.

With treads almost touching, they rammed into the brush and small trees, tearing the berms apart and exposing the NVA hiding in them. They charged up the slope with all weapons blazing. The long nineties were punching out an indiscriminate mix of H.E., cannister, and even an occasional smoke round.

The gunners were shooting so fast that the loaders could only grab what came to hand, hoping it was the right thing. The co-ax switches were left on; when a gunner loosed one of the cannon shells, he traversed his sights, keeping the triggers down until the main gun was ready again.

The drivers rammed and trampled groups of fleeing NVA, as the fire from the turrets broke their nerve, flushing them from cover. When the Recon tracks pulled up level with the heavier vehicles, the shells from the nineties endangered them; so the battle was continued with machine guns only, the .50s and M60s from the tracks making up for the loss of cannister.

The enemy troops were so thoroughly panicked that they had little thought of resistance. The loaders, freed from having to feed the nineties, picked up submachine guns and sacks of grenades and, popping in and out of their hatches, they joined in the fray. Even the drivers, remembering their old tricks from Bong Son, would crack the hatches and nail one or two from off the top of a brush pile using .45s.

"Where did you people learn to fight like this?" the MP sergeant asked me. "I saw one tank commander swing his gun over the rear deck, knock some NVA off the engine covers and down into the weeds. He threw a frag after them for good measure, and then machine-gunned two more who were attempting to get a rocket into his buddy's running gear.

"It was a slaughterhouse." His face was showing the shock of the violence, as he went on. "One minute we were scared shitless, and the next it was like wolves were loose in the sheepfold. The NVA weren't acting much like soldiers. All they wanted to do was get away from those tiger-faced mothers."

The radio came to life: "Roadrunner, this is Chopper 5." It was the exec's call number. "Put my ammo sergeant on the air."

The MP handed me the mike and, not having an official call sign, I said, "Five, this is Zippo. Do you want the load up there yet?"

"Roger that. There's a platoon of gunships coming out. Wait until you hear their rockets, then come on up."

I could already hear the unmistakable sound of heavy cavalry-in-the-sky, so I heaved myself up into the ring mount. "All right Rich, break's over. Let's go up and see what else they've torn up."

As we drove up over the rise, we heard the wham-thump of tank guns, as 3d Platoon "sanitized" the trees across the valley. Gazing over the battlefield, I could see why they hadn't been able to get to the other side. The enemy commander was a damned cagey man. He'd put his staging area and reserve forces on a hill north of the ambush site and across a swampy area that looked as though it could absorb an entire company of tanks.

The security infantry from Schueller were trucked in, more were airlifted in, and they were working their way up that hill. They were supported by some of the Scout tracks, while 2d Platoon tried to find a way around the obstacle. That was one smart officer; but he'd been out-foxed and outshot, and the majority of his men were now a bloody mess on the slope below him.

The tanks had made a "U" formation and, as we drove into this, another slid across the gap, sealing us in. The turrets were still firing, and empty shell casings were flying as the loaders cleaned house. A squad of infantry detailed as ground security swarmed aboard the truck, and shells and belts began disappearing into the tanks. Soon they were resupplied, and we made ready to get out of there.

The exec, who'd been examining bodies and equipment, came over with two enemy soldiers in his trailer who were more-or-less alive—they had been interrogated.

"What we're fighting," he announced, "is most of the NVA 95B Regimental Combat Team. The infantry is in their staging area and reports finding *tons* of abandoned plunder. This is only half the ambush, though; they were planning to hit both ends of the convoy and then chop it up at leisure, so we'll have to find the rest of the buggers and bounce them out of their holes."

Turning to me, he said, "Sarge, take your rig down to the original site where it's safer, and set up to resupply 2d and the infantry."

The tank box opened up to let us out and we burned rubber off that hill. There was some sporadic sniping, and we had a lot of sensitive demolition material on board. Second Platoon came out of the woods on schedule, so we resupplied them, the infantry, and the few tracks that were still around, with ammo.

With that job finished, we scrounged up an escort and headed back to Schueller, before the other half of the NVA force could get into position. Sergeant Ferguson's 2-5 tank was shepherding us back to the firebase when, suddenly, it stopped dead in the road, spun in its tracks, and rolled up next to us.

"You're only half a klick out now," Ferguson said. "Somolik and the Scouts just dug into the rest of that regiment—see ya later!" And he took off in a large cloud of dust.

Looking back towards the scene of the morning's combat, I could see the meat grinder starting up again. Gunships were clattering up out of An Khe, and an air strike was in progress. It was going to be a bad day all 'round for Regiment 95B.

Back at the firebase, we found a lot of hasty digging and sandbagging going on. The "rear area" troops were making ready for one of the NVA's spite attacks. When driven off a target, they had a nasty tendency to pick another objective and give it a pasting—just to show they were still in the war. As we came through the gate, I noticed that Sanchez and Kennet had the spare machine gun set up on top of our bunker, and that the 6-tank had been towed to where its turret could cover the open field across from the base.

Cheyenne was in the habit of using his command radios to monitor the goings-on of the brass, and anybody else whose frequency he discovered. He came over.

"The body count is up to three hundred and rising."

"Well, what good's that gonna do us?" I asked. "From what folks back in the States have been writing us, the news people would rather believe the North Viets than our own officers."

Cheyenne grinned. "We got the goods on 'em this time. Biggio and the infantry captain are having the bodies dragged out of the hills and counted. And they're stacking them by the side of the road so they can be photographed."

"Lots-a-luck," I said, pessimistically. "Remember downtown Pleiku, when, after we were gone, they photographed the holes *I* made with the main gun in that building and credited it to the VC? I haven't seen a reporter or a cameraman since I hit the country and that's been damn near ten months now. Where in the hell are they getting the stories they're telling back home?"

Richardson, Kennet, Sanchez, and I put in a damn busy day, and, once we had made the necessary preparations for a night attack, we crawled into our bunker and passed out, leaving the night watch up to Cheyenne and the rest of the Widowmaker's crew. We slept way past breakfast but, at around 1000, hunger woke us. When we came out of the bunker, we were facing a pile of dead NVA approximately twelve feet in diameter and easily six feet high.

"What in the name of the ancient gods is going on?" I wanted to know.

"Calm down, Zippo," Black said. "The infantry dropped 'em off on their way back to An Khe last night. They're for show-and-tell. The Old Man's called all the news services and the Army Information people, so they could see what we're doing out here."

"Hey Sarge," Sanchez called. "The grunts already got all the good stuff." He was sitting on top of the pile of corpses, going through their packs, searching for the inevitable American magazine centerfolds, the northern flags, or other trophies.

"Come on down from there," I hollered. "Black says the cooks saved some chow for the working soldiers."

Wham! Wham! Wham! The best damn mortar gunner I ever saw got the mess hall, the showers, and the latrine with his first three shots—and our day was off to a galloping start. My first thought was that the VC must be on a hill located a few hundred yards south of the LZ. But that didn't make sense because our ammo dump was on that side, and a forward observer could see into it, and would have tried to blow our supplies first.

The gunner's pattern was beginning to "walk" across the base. By analyzing the shape of the explosion, I could see that he was shooting from somewhere west of us, because most of the blast went east, away from the direction of shell travel.

Sanchez had spotted the impact "flower" too, and was scanning the slightly overcast sky, attempting to pick up the black dot of incoming rounds. He wasn't having any luck, since the actual point of impact was off to the side of us. At this point, Lieutenant Walker came up with a track mechanic named Doverspike and an ancient 60mm mortar tube that he'd liberated from a retreating ARVN company.

The tube had been kicking around for a couple of months, but we had no base plate, bipod, or even ammo for it, so I'd forgotten that the gun existed.

"We got some ammo for it by swapping the door guns off a downed chopper to an SF command team," Walker explained.

"Yeah, fine," I said. "But what good is it with no bipod or base plate?"

"Well, they can be hand-held," Doverspike put in, "and I heard somewhere that a helmet full of rocks will take the recoil."

"Thanks a lot, Spike. Let's give it a try. Where's a good spot?"

"How about between our bunker and that pile of bodies," Sanchez said. Filling his steel pot with rocks, he set it on the ground while Doverspike and I unpacked some cases of H.E.

By now, Kennet had the map out and was going over it with Sanchez. "Look at this, Zippo," he said, laying the map on the dirt beside the mortar. "There's a shelf right behind that ridge on the other side of the valley, west and a tad north, just in line with that bus down there."

"Uh-huh, 280 degrees and about eighteen hundred yards; max range for that 60mm he's using—and for this one, too. Let's set up at charge four and pay that bastard back for ruining breakfast."

Forget about that helmet full of rocks. The breech ball punched through into highlands hardpan, and went down about ten inches before it stopped. Once it packed in, though, I could "steer" it with light taps, protecting my hands with an insulated loader's mitt. After six rounds, it stabilized, and we walked the point of impact over the ridge and started to traverse, hoping to get close enough to jar the enemy gunner. Doverspike, who'd burned his hands while we were first settling the tube in, came back bandaged up, and we traded off on gun duty.

I'd put in some time on howitzers back in '61, so indirect fire wasn't exactly a new thing for me, and there was just enough overcast to let me see the shells leaving and the point of impact. We didn't expect to do much except raise our own morale, but suddenly the incoming fire stopped. As we were congratulating ourselves, it started up again, working its way across the field towards *us*.

"Hey Sarge," someone yelled, "that means his forward observer can see in here."

"Right. You guys get in the bunker; this is a good time

to go for the rest of the shells." The Old Man's jeep was sitting in front of the command bunker, and I jumped in, hit the starter, and took off before the NVA gunner could shift targets again.

As I drove by the remains of the latrine, he resumed his pattern—right where he'd left off. (If that guy is still alive, I'd like to take lessons from him.) The pattern was working back and forth across the base, and I had to stop and let it cross in front of me before I could get back to our bunker with the ammo. Mortars, like lightning, seldom strike twice in the same place, so I just followed the shell holes. As I raced by the command bunker, the exec stuck his head out and shouted, "We're not gonna forget this one, Zippo."

"He hasn't moved his tube," Kennet said; "not enough time."

"Right," I said, "you and Sanchez get a dozen each unpacked and unsafetied. We'll blow his doors off—and then jump in the bunker."

At about this time, Cheyenne Black spotted an antenna sticking out of that bus down in the valley. He ran over to the 105 battery that shared the base with us, and I saw one of the guns begin to depress its muzzle.

With two loaders feeding it, that little mortar tube could really pump it out—all I had to do was tap it lightly to ensure dispersion. Halfway through our minibarrage, the howitzer lobbed a shell into the bus and, as we fired our last few rounds, all incoming fire ceased.

Afterward, some desk jockey in An Khe actually had the nerve to order an investigation to find out whether there had been any hostiles on the bus. Luckily, they found the radio parts; otherwise, the gunner could have been court-martialed. . . . What a "Mickey Mouse" way to run a war.

* * *

The blame for erroneous body counts should not rest on the military services. We tried everything we knew to get some coverage of the battle. There were thirty NVA corpses in a secure perimeter—all stacked, uniformed, and tabulated as to rank—ready for the camera. And out at the ambush site, there were about three hundred more—all obviously NVA, and just as obviously killed by Americans. By then, we'd heard from news media that the Tet offensive had been a disaster, and that we were supposed to be losing. So our commanders decided to set up the proof and let reporters come out and count the bodies themselves.

Not one news reporter or cameraman showed.

Three days is the limit in that kind of climate and when one of the decedents winked at me, it was time to get rid of the dead.

"Take the jeep, Sarge," the Old Man said. "There's a dozer digging a trench down in the valley."

I tied them in pairs to the trailer hitch and, with Kennet driving, we hauled them out. On each trip, two Coca-Cola girls, who were peddling their drinks outside the gate, pointed and giggled, giving us big smiles. It was nice to know that somebody appreciated your efforts.

Part of the way through the detail, when we stopped to buy Cokes from the girls, the exec came out and made us drape a poncho over the bodies behind us. "So they won't shock the girls," he explained.

Since the official chroniclers of the war had shown no interest in our victory, the CO asked me to take some pictures for him—before, during, and after cremation—for the company records. So, while the rest of the men were eating their lunch, I took quite a few shots. But the PX film lab must not have liked them, because when that roll came back, those seven pictures were blacked out.

Photographs and credit notwithstanding, we had once again done our job. The NVA had lost an entire battalion, from colonel to cook, and the road to the highlands was open. (The 69th opened up that road, and the 69th kept it open until they were withdrawn from Nam in 1970.) With the retrieval of the Lurp team, the battle for control of An Khe Pass was over.

The score: NVA—approximately three hundred killed; Americans—one. This took place on 10, 11, and 12 April 1968, about fifteen kilometers west of An Khe on Highway 19E. On the last day, NVA Regiment 95B ceased to exist as a fighting force. It did not make the television news.

Chapter Sixteen

A BRAND
NEW TOY

The exec was careful to stand upwind of us when we came in from the cremation detail.

"I've got two pieces of good news for you," he said. "First, the shower's been fixed. Second, your new tank is sitting in the ordnance depot at Qui Nhon, so you can unbury those hidden supplies and unauthorized weapons, and go pick it up."

Sanchez, Kennet, and I must have looked worried, because the lieutenant said, "Nobody finked on you. But I've been watching Zippo for damn near a year now, and that dozer tank acquired some strange capabilities just after you took it over. For one thing, that tank has been seen shooting machine guns in three directions at the same time—accurately, and at night. That means it has at least one extra machine gun and several extra night-vision scopes." (To be exact, we had two extra guns,

202

and one starlight scope, and two pairs of infrared binoculars, traded for a case of Southern Comfort.)

"Er, yes sir," I said, somewhat embarrassed.

"Don't sweat it, Sarge," he said with a grin. "Just keep the goodies hidden when the Old Man's around." That was the exec's friendly way of warning us that the captain was going to hold an equipment inspection.

But that was no problem; the extra hardware would rest in its normal hiding places, under the righthand 90mm racks, on top of the fuel tanks, and behind the batteries. There are other places, but they'll remain secret for the benefit of present tank crews.

The next morning, we loaded our personal gear, leftover tank equipment, those "unauthorized goodies" and a basic load of ammo into the company supply truck, and tagged on to an east-bound convoy. The six-by was headed into Qui Nhon anyway, and it felt good to be temporarily fancy-free and to leave the driving and responsibility to someone else.

The ordnance section was, in effect, a giant equipment park, loaded with machinery of all descriptions, and we had to find a guide to locate the new Executioner for us.

"Here she is," he said, proud as a car salesman. "Brand new, not a rebuild."

"Hey look," Kennet said. "She's got fenders! You won't be getting mud down your neck anymore, Sarge." Now that was something I could really appreciate. Tracks throw an unbelievable amount of crud, and fenders are the first casualties of jungle busting.

New fenders weren't the only nice things. There'd been a modification on this tank, something that every tank needed. Since the tank commander sometimes has to go through entire firefights with his head out, ducking rockets and scanning into the bushes, we had requested some sort of improved vision area, something like the M85 cupola on the M60 tank.

Instead, they had cast up an armored ring with half a dozen seven-inch, bulletproof windows in it. I still had the "idiot-mount" .50 to work around, but now, for the first time in nearly a year, I could see out without chancing sudden decapitation.

Like kids with a new toy, we climbed all over the tank, checking for new features or hidden flaws. We brought aboard our own personalized helmets and other gear, and it took only a few minutes to load everything we'd brought. Then, rather than leave the tank in the ordnance park, we drove it to the base's transient barracks, drawing quite a few stares. We intended to get a fairly early start in the morning.

Not trusting the techs who had set the vehicle up, we began the day by checking all the end connectors, and giving all external lube points a shot of grease. Then we fueled up and rolled out to the gunnery range to synchronize the gun/sight linkage.

"We haven't got a boresight board," the range NCO said, "so you'll have to set your sights the long way."

"No sweat," I replied. "We'll be synchroed and gone in about half an hour."

"What? This I gotta see," he said. "That's supposed to be an all-day job."

The normal procedure for this task is to tape string "cross hairs" on the gun muzzle itself, and then partially disassemble the breech, so you can sight through the gun at some distant object. Next, you move all the sight reticles to the same point of aim, and start zero firing each weapon. The sight adjustment can also be done with a specially-marked board that fastens to the muzzle, but we had evolved a faster method—because house ramming tends to foul up gun alignment.

We'd liberated a length of 4×4 from a street sign in front of the transient barracks, and now Kennet drove us out onto the firing range, reading the distance off the odometer; it was roughly three-quarters of a mile. Sanchez and I sledged the aiming stake in and, using the range finder, I backed us off exactly one thousand yards.

The trick is you must know the exact characteristics of your shells—there is a card in the ammo crate that gives the exact elevation necessary for any given distance. We turned off the turret motor and put the proper elevation on the gun, using a bubble level known as a gunners' quadrant.

Sanchez, still using manual controls, fired three rounds while I acted as loader. After relaying the sights to the top of the stake, we just moved all the little adjustable reticles or cross hairs to where the projectiles had actually hit. One more experimental round lifted the 4×4 out and sent it into orbit; we left one dumbfounded range noncom staring at four holes, shaking his head.

On the outskirts of Qui Nhon proper, there was a small compound that contained, among other things, a PX. Since this was a brand-new tank, it was missing some of the amenities—such as a beer cooler—so we needed to do a little shopping. Tanks always attract attention, and we were drawing the familiar complement of stares as we pulled into the gravel parking lot, being very careful not to tear up the ground with sharp turns. In fact, we prided ourselves on our ability to maneuver these big, clumsy machines anywhere, without damaging anything—unless we intended to.

Our shopping list was sizable, including film, candy, beer, magazines, and more, so we were inside for quite a while. When we came out, the Vietnamese manager was standing beside the tank, fuming.

"You no bring tank in this parking lot. Place for wheel vehicle only!" he insisted as we loaded our purchases. He was steadily getting madder and feeding on his own rage, as we ignored him.

I could see that Sanchez was beginning to get hot, too, and was almost to the point of punching him. "Easy Roman," I whispered, "we'll fry his bacon on the way out." Kennet had already cranked up as I mounted onto the hull. Then the PX manager put his foot in it.

"No no, you stay. I call MPs. You GI in plenty hot water now."

"Kennet."

"Yeah Sarge, I heard him."

"Neutral steer, hard right, full throttle—exactly like you were on top of a bunker."

Three times the dozer tank spun in its own length, grinding twelve inches into the ground with each turn. Finally, we heaved up out of a hole big enough to hide a small truck, and drove out the gate, leaving the manager jumping in frustrated rage.

This wasn't my day for "winning the hearts and minds of the people." No sooner had we cleared the congestion of the built-up area, than we got stuck behind a Lambretta ditty wagon tooling along at about ten miles an hour. The eight passengers in the back were all pointing at the tank and shouting at the driver, who was hunched over his handlebars. He was hogging the middle of the lane, and refused to pull over to let us pass.

There was a steady stream of oncoming traffic and a soft rice paddy on each side, so I decided to use one of Hazelip's tricks.

"Kennet, ease up till the gun tube is next to his cab."

Once the muzzle was level with the driver, I used the override to give him a solid tap with the blast deflector. Like most people, after getting his full attention, he was remarkably easy to reason with. He moved over—to the obvious relief of his passengers.

No one was expecting us to hurry with a new, untried machine, so we took our time ascending into the highlands, stopping to check the tracks, oil levels, and bearings. We'd nursed a cripple for so long that constant checking was second nature to us. And it was difficult to adjust to the fact that the tank wasn't going to fall apart with no warning.

With time to kill, we stopped off at each of 1st Platoon's one-tank garrisons, passing the time of day and doing some blade work, improving their fortifications and showing off our new baby.

Once we were within radio range of company firebase, I checked in and received orders to wait outside the main gate of An Khe base for the ammo-fuel trucks, which would be making a run.

"I got a feelin' about this, Sarge," Kennet said.

"Uh-huh," Sanchez put in, "I think we're gonna be escorting supplies all over the company's area."

"Well, look at it this way," I told them. "It would keep us out of base most of the time, but still allow us to have mess-hall meals, and a shot at the PX and NCO club every once in a while."

Our gut feeling turned out to be accurate. When not out replacing a cripple, we spent a lot of time shepherding trucks, and doing blade work. A dozer tank is a functional part of a tank company, but a lot of our time was spent on an engineer "waiting list" to get normal work done. For example, several of the back-country ravines had made tedious detours necessary because they were too deep and steep for tanks to traverse, and too far back for a regular dozer to get to. As a result, we were "running around loose."

"There's Recon now," Sanchez said as, escorted by

one of Somolik's far-ranging ACAVs, we crashed out of a hilly, second-growth forest, into a sloping meadow. The cleared part had once been the site of a Montagnard village—the foundation posts were still visible. The Recon tracks were drawn up in a circular night laager. Lieutenant Somolik came over and climbed up on our fender.

"There's a regular gulch inside the treeline over there," he said, pointing to the south side of the field, "about a ten-foot drop, with a level bottom, and a vertical wall on the other side."

"Well, let's go and see," I said, dropping off the fender. "Sanchez, take over and tuck inside the laager for a while."

We'd been escorting the roving supply section, when the Old Man had come on the radio, to make sure my explosive racks were full. Then he had given us one of those "for Americans only" codes that drove Charlie nuts. "Recon has an obstacle, and you're to rendezvous Jack Benny east of company base with an ACAV that will lead you in." ("Jack Benny" meant thirty-nine kilometers.)

Now, looking down at the obstacle, I was estimating how much work it would take to put through an impromptu roadway.

"Of course the local VC will try to mine it after we're through," Somolik said, "but we've got our own mine detectors now. And the Lurps will keep an eye on it, out of general principles."

"Right, sir. I think we can have you through here in a few hours."

"Isn't that a bit optimistic, Zippo? What are you going to use on that dirt wall on the other side? I thought you'd need a few of my men to dig bore holes to blast out the wall."

"Maybe you'd better line up a detail, at that," I relented, "but I think we can adapt one of the bunker-busting techniques and use the ninety to undercut it."

"Well go ahead, then. I'll dismount two squads for security."

Operating on my hand signals, Kennet dropped the blade about thirty feet back from the edge and made the starting cut. The idea was to gradually notch out the near wall by pushing dirt into the ravine until the vertical drop became a twenty-five-degree slope. It took ten passes before we were satisfied. Then I got in the turret and addressed the far wall.

Cutting from the bottom isn't nearly as easy as a top cut, but we'd been figuring out a new procedure—and this was the time to try it. Since we still were without a loader, Sanchez fed the gun and I shot from the override. Four delay shells ate a hole in the bottom of the wall; and then the blade tore a huge gap, undercutting the bank. After four more shots, enough dirt fell to let us get the bow up for another bite.

We did another series, then backed up and hit the improvised ramp at full throttle, using momentum to push the blade through the last four feet. We rose to a hair-raising angle; then, covered with dirt, rocks, vines, and brush, we settled back to level on top of the bank. A few more cuts dressed up the surface—and we had created another pass.

"Pretty goddamn slick, Sarge," the lieutenant said. "I've been on the horn to Captain Biggio. You're to stay with us till we come out of the hills east of An Khe, near that Korean base."

"Yes sir. What kind of operation do you have here anyway?"

"It's a combined sweep; we keep two tracks as headquarters, and you'll stay with us. The other twelve are split into groups of four, each working a ridge or valley, and linking up with foot patrols from the 173d. We try to get back together at night, but sometimes a section gets stalled and takes a day or two to catch up. That's one of the reasons for keeping you around for a while—the other reason is that long ninety.''

I was beginning to see where the term ''grunt'' came from. It was the sound made as the overburdened infantryman picked up the seventy-pound pack with which the powers-that-be had loaded him. We would see those poor ground-pounders chuffing up a hill, carrying packs as big as their chests, wrapped up in flak jackets, sweating rivers—and breathing like engines.

I'm not claiming to be an expert, but I go back to the old ''brown boot'' Army, and the forty-pound pack. I've been a paratrooper in the same division these guys were in, and had the same jungle training, and unless these kids were a lot stronger than the youth of the '50s, that extra thirty pounds could only detract from their effectiveness.

The combat infantryman is the reason that the rest of the military exists. Even the USS *New Jersey*, or a B-52, is only smoothing the way for the man with the bayonet. The only way any war gets won is for the combat troop to walk into enemy HQ. This is especially true in a guerrilla war. He has to go into those jungles and drag the bastards out.

Throughout my year in Vietnam, the tanks hauled tons of excess infantry baggage, just to give the troopers a break—a pack mule is not an effective combatant. That seems to be a cycle of history, though. The longer the time is between wars, the heavier the soldier's load gets.

As we worked our way east, roughly parallel with the highway, we moved out of the 173d zone and began meeting South Korean patrols. These soldiers, comprising the Capital Division, were a larger and stockier Asian people than the Vietnamese; and they could do a better job of boosting the local morale than could a group of Americans. Their base camps had the same degree of sophistication as ours, including refrigerators and all. But they were Asian, not Caucasian; and they could say to the Viets: "Look at us. In 1950 we were where you are now. Stick with the Americans, and you will be rich and free—because it happened to us."

Of course, we were all a wee bit naive back then. We hadn't realized that the news networks seemed to have developed a symbiotic relationship with pot-brained street freaks, and would influence a publicity-happy Congress to all but sell their souls—while using our bodies— just for some camera time.

After Recon had covered its assigned territory, they headed back up the road for a refit at company base—and another sweep. But we got orders to replace one of 1st Platoon's tanks, which had taken some hits in an attack on its strong point. So, as the ACAVs lined up and moved west, we unloaded our Korean infantry and took off down the highway.

We met the 1st Platoon tank on our way down from the highlands; the TC handed me his range card and map as we sat, side by side on the highway.

"It's a nice location," he told me, standing on the fender of his smoking, trembling mount. "That hill behind you isn't nearly as close as it looks. There's no place where they can defilade a mortar, but now and then a few rockets will come whistling in."

"Well then, what happened to you," I wanted to know.

"A 57mm up the tail," he answered, disgustedly, "while I was out looking around. The two left-rear cylinders got knocked out of line. The gunners who did it aren't around anymore, though. I fed 'em a load of cannister. Well, I'll see ya later. I gotta at least try to get this wreck up to An Khe. Oh yeah,'' he added, as an afterthought, ''Black was down in Qui Nhon, and they diverted him to our strong point. He's there now, with your new loader.''

Well, glory be, I thought, fresh meat and a chance to settle back and bullshit for a while.

The minifort was just above the base of the highland foothills, and we had a view of the lowland rice paddies, with a rising green wall at our backs. It was a low, sand-bagged parapet located on a small rise beside the highway, surrounded by a single coil of concertina wire. As we circled the tank behind the rise, we could see the wire gate being dragged open by a GI and a Vietnamese boy.

Widowmaker was parked at one side of the small enclosure, which was built around a bunker and an open-sided thatch shelter. At the rear of the compound were two hastily-erected, woven-bamboo shelters from which cooking smoke was curling upwards. A dozen chickens pecked in the dust, while one of those butt-ugly Viet pigs foraged in the garbage heap outside the wire.

As soon as we shut off the engine and hopped down from the fenders, I gave the defenses a quick once-over. They were minimal, since it had been designed to be defended by a tank-in-residence. There were firing pits for about a dozen infantry, and a squad of grunts had their pup tents set up in a row in back of the low bunker.

''What in the hell is this mess?'' I asked Black, as he came up and handed me a cold beer.

''Introductions first,'' he said. ''This is Smith, your new loader.''

A well-built redhead stepped forward.

''Welcome to the crew,'' I said. ''Throw your gear up into the bustle rack; and don't ever get caught without your .45 again.''

"Right, Sarge," he said, slightly embarrassed, digging the weapon out of his bag.

"This is my new gunner," Black continued, gesturing to a handsome blond man. "He's Irish; and he's a good turret mechanic, so we can quit some of this jury-rigging."

"Howdy Sarge, my name's Harp." We shook hands; he had a bone-crusher grip, and seemed to like to test other men's strength.

Cheyenne went on to explain the situation. "The infantry is from 5th Mechanized, and they rotate in and out on a schedule of their own. The natives who live in the huts back there are refugees who have lost their villages. There are two girls, an old papa-san, and a boy. Between 'em, they cook, do laundry, run errands, and keep the place cleaned up. They've got no home to call their own, but refugees seem naturally to gravitate to a place of safety and, around here, that's one of these tank forts.

"Technically, they're not supposed to be allowed inside the compound, but we can see a long way out from here, so they just zip out to the hootches when anyone important is coming. The only problem is," he continued, "the local VC commander has sworn to 'execute' the girls for 'collaboration'—which doesn't mean shit, because he's an outlaw. But the bridge posts and strong points have been getting hit."

Black and I had been working together long enough to see eye to eye on most matters, and Company A's TCs were given much leeway, due to the responsibility we had learned to carry. It was now close to dark, so there wasn't enough time for him to climb the range of hills before sundown; he would stay with us tonight. Unless the Widowmaker was badly needed, a few extra days wouldn't matter—and together we might be able to seriously damage a few VC.

"I'll set up on the southwest corner, Cheyenne; then

we can cover the road and that open strip with the bow gun.''

"But there ain't any bow gun on an M48," Harp cut in incredulously.

"Go look, son," Black said, and when Harp had gone, "The kid's got possibilities, but he still thinks by stateside rules. Anyhow, you're right. I'll take the south and east sides; that way, we can use each other's searchlights, and the infantry can take the north wall." The squad leader said that was fine with him, but asked if we had any spare heavy weapons he could use to back up his M16s.

"Sure, Sarge," I said. "We can fix you up with an M60 and a grenade gun for as long as we're here." He was staring at us in amazement, when Harp came back.

"You two could be jailed in the States for those tanks," he declared. "There's an extra co-ax mounted on the dozer's bow, in some kind of homemade swivel, and we've got a mortar welded to our turret." (I'd been wondering where that 60mm had ended up.)

Kennet came over, carrying the extra machine gun, and the squad leader asked whether that thing was a tank or a rolling ordnance dump.

"I dunno, Sarge," Kennet said, "but about a week after Zippo took over our original dozer tank, you couldn't take three steps without tripping over something that went boom."

For the next two days, we went discreetly about our business, trying to strengthen the perimeter without alerting an observer. Black got a relay connection with Company HQ, and got permission to stay for a few days; Somolik's expanded Recon unit was to be paired with a mounted infantry company, and they would take over security for the road, all the way up to the pass. The company was on the move again, and would pick us up on the way back to Bong Son. That outfit must have won out more pairs of tracks than did a normal tank company in the entire period of World War II.

I noticed that the Vietnamese ''camp followers'' were very anxious to make sure they were inside the wire by dark. The infantry sergeant explained, ''They're supposed to stay outside, but Charlie's been known to slip up and commit murder; one time, they booby-trapped a hootch. A girl went out to start breakfast and got blown to hell-and-gone. Bastards!

''Take that boy over there,'' he said, pointing at the kid feeding the blind, old papa-san. ''He should be in school and the boy scouts; instead he sells our trash in town and helps us scout for VC. The Cong have sworn to kill his sister—just because she does my laundry. At least the fuckers wear the right color—SS black.''

We deliberately left the girls outside until well after sundown that night, and then had them sneak back in—leaving the cook-fire burning—in hopes that the apparent lack of preparedness would encourage the Cong. The ground troops were sleeping, wrapped in their poncho liners, behind the north wall; and we had two men awake in each turret, scanning the night.

Since this wasn't a mobile operation, the two intercoms were wired together, to avoid radio leaks. Harp, using a starlight scope, spotted them first (no one is more vigilant than a new man in combat).

''Twenty men coming across the paddy,'' he whispered nervously over the intercom.

''Right,'' I said, reaching back to wake Sanchez who was sleeping on the dunnage in the bustle rack. Black was already moving around on his turret, and as Sanchez slipped into the cupola, I dropped off the hull and went over to the infantry squad.

People who live in a war zone can sense trouble. Three

pairs of eyes followed me from the bunker, watching as I crossed the tiny enclosure.

"They're out there, Sarge. About twenty so far, but that's not enough to give this place a hard time."

"Yeah," he whispered back. "There's probably more of 'em low-crawling up that low spot out there." I handed him a dozen parachute flares, just in case our turrets were busy when he needed light, and then got back to the Executioner.

Black had cranked his turret around to the east and I could hear the blowers on his searchlight. He was scanning on infrared. The IR binoculars showed another group of around twenty out there, and Sanchez, down in the gunner's position, reported a bunch to the west of us also. On impulse, I swung the turret to the north, but could see nothing at all.

Cheyenne, using his binoculars and my light, said, "That's it, Zippo. They're gonna keep our attention with those three double squads and then try to carry the north face."

"Real sophisticated tactics," Sanchez said sarcastically. "I wonder where they learned that?"

"Probably from watching cowboy movies through binoculars," Kennet put in. "Uh-oh, three of them just snuck across the road."

The hiss of an opening beer can, accompanied by a resounding belch, echoed out of Widowmaker's turret; then, as if that had been a signal, all three groups of VC opened up. Still not wanting to use white light, we let the gunners start picking them off using the infrared sights. We had the advantage of having that two-ton blade in front of us, and we had hung a pair of claymores on it.

So, after telling Kennet to keep his IR headlights and scope working, I swung the turret towards the western group. A momentary doubt shook me; they weren't immediately visible. But a closer look showed a tight cluster of prone figures about fifty yards out. (Infrared equipment gives one almost no depth perception.)

"Switch on the main gun," I ordered, picking up the M79, "I'm gonna try to goose them." We usually kept a few tear-gas rounds available, in case we wanted some survivors to talk to. This time, as the 40mm crybaby shell burst among them, the group stood up and a flechette cartridge—eight thousand steel darts—nailed the whole bunch. Simultaneously, the claymores were set off, and the bow gun let off a few bursts.

There was a pop and a shrieking sound from the infantry, and suddenly a parachute flare turned our little corner of hell into daylight. The M60 began firing in heavy bursts, using more ammo than necessary, and the ground-pounders opened up with their 5.56mm popguns. As we suspected, the main force of about fifty had been waiting on the north side; and they were a lot closer than we'd figured.

"Hey Sarge," Kennet said, "there's a few in the wire, I gotta button up." Swinging the turret, which was now on white light, I raked the concertina wire, catching three who were attempting to work their way through. Then, catching sight of a small, dark figure down behind me, I fished for a grenade. When another parachute flare lit up the place, it turned out to be one of the girls.

"Get back in that fucking bunker, you little idiot!"

"No no, gimme bullet," she said, pointing at the north wall.

Looking, I could see pajama-clad figures in the outer wire, and the MG was still firing those long, wasteful bursts. The infantryman who had been feeding the gun was now trying to bandage a bleeding shoulder. The twelve-year-old kid had taken his place at the gunner's side, and had sent his sister for more 7.62mm.

"Smith, throw me a couple more belts," I called and, pulling about a thousand rounds out of the floor boxes, he passed them up to me. Another flare went up and, as the girl ran off trailing the belts, I could see the other one, crouching beside the bunker with the stack of parachute cartridges.

By this time, the groups who had tried to draw our attention from the main attack were either dead or gone, so both turrets, both .50s, and the infantry's weapons made short work of the rest.

"Now maybe I can finish that goddamn beer," Black said—and we all cracked up, releasing pent-up nervousness. Nobody slept well that night, and we kept launching occasional M79 rounds into the dark, to keep the VC from retrieving the bodies.

The next morning, as the girls were making coffee and hunting for eggs, we took the grapnel and showed the green hands how to check bodies.

"First off," Cheyenne said, "never touch them till you've given them a good pull, because the Cong have a nasty habit of booby-trapping corpses." Suiting his action to his words, he tossed the grapnel out, hooked a rapidly stiffening bandit, and, lying down, gave it a savage jerk. Nothing happened but, taking no chances, we checked all of them that way just to be sure.

We were supposed to call Military Intelligence for that task but, since they couldn't possibly know our local situation, we'd learned to do our own "information analysis" before they arrived. For instance, one of the decedents had been a barber who made the rounds of the tank positions. We never had trusted that one; in fact, Sanchez would sit for his haircut holding a grenade with the pin pulled.

One of the girls identified another as a pimp who had tried to recruit her. The boy was eyeing one of the SKS carbines that were lying about. Most GIs would be uneasy with an armed civilian in those circumstances, but this kid and the others had proved themselves, so we merely grinned at him and walked back to breakfast, leaving him to do his shopping. After all, he had two girls and an old papa-san to protect.

Chapter Seventeen

SHORT TIMER

The Engineer Corps had finally managed to get tank-rated bridges all along Highway 1, so now we were able to drive all the way to Bong Son, instead of having to rely on sea transport. Two days after our last fight, the company came rolling down the mountain road and, after showing the ACAV crews the range cards and introducing them to the infantry squad leader and the resident Viets, we tagged onto the company.

The Old Man had already flown ahead, and was picking out a base for us. The wheeled transport, escorted by a couple of gun trucks, had already gone by, so our segment was the muscle—three platoons of M48s, the tank retriever, commo track, and the fuel and ammo section. Black put the Widowmaker into its normal place at the head of the column, and I told Kennet to cut in just ahead of the supply section. By now, the truck drivers and supply handlers were all old friends and they regarded the dozer tank as their official bodyguard.

We relaxed in the turrets as the treads ate up the miles. The plains, forests, and coasts around Bong Son were a second home to us—and we'd already proved our competence in this kind of war. Traffic was light, and an MP jeep was clearing the way ahead of us, so the drivers could take it easy too, without having to pay overly much attention to the sometimes skittish monsters.

Monsoon was over down here, but the paddies were still green. You could see girls, working with a graceful rhythm, pumping water with pitch-lined baskets. They stood on opposite sides of a pond, each with a long cord in her hand; the cords, attached to the top and bottom of the basket, were the "pump." A tug on the bottom snatched the basket down into the pool, and a pull on the top pair of cords lifted the container up to the irrigation canal, dumping two gallons of water into the paddy.

Beyond the girls, I could see water buffalo working the fields, and boys herding cows. Farther from the road, set in clumps in the green fields, were the thatch-roofed houses of the farmers. The scene was truly beautiful—and potentially lethal. Black's gravelly voice broke into my daydreaming.

"Chopper Niner, this is Seven Alpha."

"This is Niner. What's up Cheyenne?"

"When you get to the next curve, look for a couple of girls with a cooler and a sun umbrella. They're probably okay, but there's one of those cocky little pricks with a motorbike by them, and I can't tell whether he's NVA, or just a pimp." We were never completely off guard, so Sanchez had automatically slipped down into the gunner's seat. Smitty appeared nervous, and I had to reassure him that we were just "checking assholes."

"I see him," Sanchez said. "Look for a man with a

red-and-grey moped and a sun helmet.'' As the column progressed, I could see the man who had been picked out with the powerful sights. The girls were distinctly jittery, and I thought I could see the outline of a notebook in one of the guy's shirt pockets. The girls must have been pumping water until recently, because the basket and ropes lay neatly curled up behind their cooler.

The man was sitting astride the moped, and I decided to have some fun. We deliberately ran the turret-motor down and, as the tank passed the girls, I waved and smiled, then swung the gun tube, causing the usual hideous hydraulic shriek. The arrogance on the man's face was replaced by sheer terror, as he frantically kicked the engine into life and took off—straight into the irrigation pond.

''See what I mean?'' I told Smitty. ''He's been in combat against tanks before. That sound means death to him.''

The ''tigers'' were back in Bong Son. The people were waving and boys were running alongside the tracks as Company A rumbled through the town. We recognized our favorite policeman, and he waved and pointed to the club, pantomiming the motion of draining a cool one.

Here and there, you could see a resentful stare, or a calculating look—Charlie was back in the ring for another bout, and something new had been added. Some VC units, like the bunch south of Pleiku, were sign-happy; one of the tank commanders up ahead in the line put out a general broadcast.

''We're famous, gentlemen. There's a wanted poster on the shrine by the old school.''

Picking up the binoculars, I could see what he was talking about. A yard-square sign with a picture of a tank in the middle was nailed to the side of a travelers' shrine. The caption read: WANTED, DEAD OR ALIVE, ANY TANK

COMMANDER FROM COMPANY A, 1ST BATTALION, 69TH
ARMOR.

"Chintzy bastards didn't give a price," one of the TCs
said, talking over the command net.

"They're most likely waiting to grade all you ama-
teurs," Black said, kidding the new men who had won
their spurs in the highlands.

Our new tank park, in a tree-shaded corner of LZ English, was much more comfortable than the old location
below the airstrip. Its only problem was it backed right up
to the fence, and some of the tank slots were within a long
grenade throw of the wire.

The small GI-oriented settlement was backed up to the
wire too, so it was convenient to buy booze, and handle
laundry and other transactions, straight over the boundary,
without having to go to the trouble of getting a pass.

The pass system was just about obsolete in that company, anyway; the crews were so responsible and loyal that
they could simply be turned loose in the knowledge that
they'd come running when needed. In fact, the outfit had
developed traditions and an identity entirely separate from
its commanders and parent organization. Being literally
bounced around from pillar to post had made us a self-
reliant group of competent, deadly professionals.

In no other army in the world could a company commander order a buck sergeant tank boss off on his own,
sometimes a hundred miles and two or three weeks away
from supervision. We tried to stay in pairs, but it wasn't
unusual for a ground CO to see a lone tank come crunch-
ing out of a forest.

Now the company was split up again, with 2d Platoon
in the northern end of our area, operating out of LZ
Apache; 1st was kept fairly close to Bong Son City and
LZ English, while 3d went out with the infantry, patrolling
and sweeping the inland plain out by Geronimo.

Some of the tanks were very old, some with as many as 17,000 miles on them. Black and I were kept busy replacing cripples, escorting the VTR, and sometimes towing in damaged vehicles ourselves. One 1st Platoon tank, making too sharp a turn, broke through the surface of a still-wet paddy, and before he gave up, the hull and half the turret were below ground level.

I was sent out to escort the retriever and, when we arrived at the scene, the platoon had set up in a hamlet and the men were hauling supplies and ammo out of the buried hull, attempting to lighten it. It took the whole platoon to haul the retriever's winch cable out to the luckless machine, but even then we were twenty feet short. A pair of tank cables had to be linked to the end, but eventually we got the tank connected to the retriever and the winch began putting a strain on the cable. At first, nothing moved; then, with the engine putting out all twelve hundred horses, the VTR started to slide forward—off the hamlet mound and out into the paddy!

Suction under the hull had locked the half-buried tank solidly in place. So now we had to get creative. By bringing the dozer up behind the retriever and burying its blade, we doubled the traction, linking the two vehicles with cables. We then pushed a pound of TNT down under the belly of the mired monster and, with a full strain on the winch, we set off the charge. It worked! The vehicle heaved up out of a self-dug pit.

After escorting the retriever back to English, we received orders to run up to 2d Platoon's location and free the 2-4 tank to come back for general maintenance and a new set of tracks. Sergeant Taylor, the platoon honcho, was sitting on his turret when we arrived, the rest of the crew cleaning the air screens and oil filters, getting ready to move. Kennet pulled us across behind the tank's hull, ready to take over the bridge-guard position when Taylor moved out.

"You'd better never leave that tank unguarded, Zippo," Taylor said, as he stepped over to our back deck, "or somebody'll sneak aboard and steal that pretty 'vision ring.' "

"Yeah," I said. "Neat isn't it? I can see 360 without getting out. I still have to poke my head out to see down next to the hull, though, so it ain't a cure-all. Have you had any decent action up here?"

"Nothing serious," he replied, carefully watching my face, "except a Chinese submarine." After we all quit shouting, he explained. Here's the story.

Division intelligence had received confirmed reports of high-ranking northern officials, and sensitive equipment being delivered by submarine. With our reputation for murderously accurate gunnery, it was natural to pick one of A Company's roving marauders for a hit. Lieutenant Walker, now the permanent commander of 2d Platoon, was sent to the coast with a nautical chart attached to his terrain map, and with orders to maintain infrared surveillance. For a start, he picked a headland that jutted into the sea, close to the reported area.

The entire country was under a sundown-to-sunrise rural curfew at the time, so he could feel free to zap anything that moved after dark. Since the fishermen depended for their livelihood on night fishing, they received a special dispensation. They could fish all night, but were not to try to change their locations. With his light section back on the road guarding bridges, the lieutenant had only three guns to work with; he spaced them across the crest of the hill, watching the fishing sampans going out, and waiting for dark.

Just past midnight, one of the men on watch heard a strange noise and woke the lieutenant. Listening closely, he could hear the buk . . . buk . . . buk of one of those single-cylinder Japanese diesels that seem to be the main source of propulsion in this part of the world.

"That's no submarine," the lieutenant said, "but it ain't supposed to be moving either. All units: infrared, normal power," he whispered into his mike. Whatever it was, the vessel skated tantalizingly just at the edge of the IR's reach.

They could hear it slowly working its way down the line of fishermen, so Walker decided to use white light. The instant he gave the order, three blue-white beams lashed out and ripped the night to shreds. First one, then the other two, caught movement—and then a one-hundred-foot coastal freighter was pinned in the beams.

"Fire a shot across his bow," Walker ordered. The 2-5 tank lashed out with an H.E.P. round dead amidships, and the freighter blew to splinters and sank.

"Goddammit, I said *across* his bow," Walker roared.

"Well he picked up speed and ran into it," the TC said defensively.

"He was right," the lieutenant later told me. "Just as the lights hit, we heard his engine almost triple its beat; but I could just see myself being court-martialed for blowing up a legal freighter. Next morning, though, we found the beach littered with supplies, including uniforms and replacement rifle stocks and bandages—so we were home free. We never did spot that sub; maybe blowing that freighter scared it off."

After finishing his story, Sergeant Taylor and his crew took off for company base, and we made ready for the night. The guard tanks operated in pairs, one directly on a bridge, and the other at some high point that allowed him to dominate a larger area. There was a subtle dirty trick in this, because we knew that the hostiles would try to mine the high parking spot after the tank had left it and come in to pair up with the bridge guardian at night.

The other tank was situated on the remains of an old, wrecked, railroad viaduct, and before he came down, I ranged on him and recorded the data for night use. Periodically, during the night, we would swing the turret to the place where the other tank parked during the day, hoping to catch some unwary VC setting a mine.

There was wreckage like that viaduct all over Vietnam, I reflected. The communist method of "liberating" a country is to destroy its power plants, blow the railroads, burn the temples, and murder the teachers and other dissidents—all in the name of the people. Then when the local army is spread to hell and back chasing "reformers," an outside force, in this case the NVA, comes in and jumps it.

When the other tank came down, we set up side by side, but facing in opposite directions, thus effectively blocking the road. This was always a time of apprehension, because several types of unpleasantness could arrive with no warning. A particularly good sniper could nail someone at sunrise or sunset. After full dark, a rocket could come whistling out of a paddy, or a mortar crew could take you under fire, forcing you to move while a demo squad mined the bridge.

But we had some countermeasures for these tricks. Harassment and interdiction helped a lot, and one of our daily tasks was to set booby traps under the bridge to catch anyone who might start sneaking around down there. In this kind of situation, we added submachine gun bursts into the bushes to our normal H&I, and we rolled occasional grenades under the bridge. Naturally, we also made out a full range card before sundown, and since those nineties can reach eight miles, one tank can make a large area very uncomfortable.

After a breakfast cooked over burning balls of C4 explosive (you could use TNT, but the smoke got into the food, altering the taste), we split up—one tank taking the high spot and the other pulling back off the roadway, parking next to the bridge. If a National Police squad chose your bridge to operate a check-point, there was a break in the monotony—a portion of the traffic was always VC. We couldn't consistently detect guerrillas in the population, but the police were experts at it; when a squad of NPs showed up, there was action.

The police, very natty in tailored, tiger-stripe fatigues, would show up shortly after daybreak, riding in a three-quarter ton with a machine gun. Their procedure was to set up a choke point on the road, and deflect selected individuals over to inspection teams. (There were no female police; if a woman was to be searched, the men did it.)

One time our attention was drawn by a rising yammer of voices. We saw a middle-aged man on a motorbike "read out" the policeman who had accosted him, and drive through the choke point. Sanchez reached for a grease gun to fire a warning burst, but a pair of strategically-placed police had the matter in hand. One of them stepped towards the man, causing him to swerve across the road to where another cop stood. The second policeman simply stuck a length of iron pipe in the spokes of the front wheel, and after the crash, he picked up the would-be escapee and frog-marched him back to the commander.

They found a lot of paperwork and money in those saddlebags, and the police immediately got on the radio. Shortly thereafter, a chopper landed and took the courier away. We watched the episode carefully; it was very interesting. Quite a bit of the loose cash, as well as one

228

valuable motorbike, was in the truck and under canvas before the helicopter landed.

Two days later, with Sergeant Taylor on the way back, we were getting ready to replace one of the 3d Platoon's weary warriors, when the radio cut into the normal routine.

"Check-point One Five, repeat, One Five; Chopper Niner or 2-3, this is Chopper 6, over."

Being only a temporary replacement, we let the platoon tank answer. He was told that a suspected courier/paymaster was leaving a village to the north of us, driving a black Citroen sedan, and was asked could he apprehend without killing. The TC stalled, saying he had to check the map, and switched over to the "bullshit frequency" buried down in the middle of the artillery band.

"Whaddaya think, Zippo? I can't get through the paddies yet, and that Citroen is faster than a tank." My mind was searching for alternatives, when Sanchez keyed his mike.

"We were over that way with Hiemes about a year ago. Since the courier can't leave the road at this time of year, blow the road in front and behind him and he's gift wrapped."

"Roger, thanks, Roman. That's all I need," and he switched back to the "authorized channels." We could barely see what was going on, since we were at road level, but the 2-3 tank was up on the railroad viaduct, fifty feet higher.

A black dot seemed to crawl along a faint brown line out in the fields, and a lazy red tracer, the mark of the 90mm shell, curved out to meet it. We could hear the muzzle blast of the gun as two more shells descended on the rural one-lane road—then the dot began backing frantically. Three more H.E. rounds dropped gracefully behind the car, and the TC came up on the command frequency.

"He's all yours, Cap'n. He ain't goin' anyplace." It wasn't long before two choppers descended on the car, stayed for about half an hour, then lifted out.

With Sergeant Taylor back in place, we moved south, headed for a road that would give us access to the section of the plain that 3d Platoon was infesting. We needed to get south of the ridgeline that supported LZ Geronimo, to avoid a lot of unnecessary mountain climbing. Rather than hurry, we split the trip into two days, spending the night with one of 1st Platoon's road guards, who was glad for the company; then we struck off cross-country.

There were platoon- and company-sized groups of infantry scattered throughout the vicinity, and each one could tell us roughly where they thought the tanks were working. I finally reached the platoon leader on the radio, just as Kennet spotted fresh tank tracks, and we homed in on them.

This region was 3d's old stomping ground. Most of the TCs and crews remembered the individual villages and could recognize some of the few remaining inhabitants. We were running into more traces of NVA; the main-force VC had been smashed as a military force in the Tet disaster. The northerners were setting up in half-abandoned hamlets and villages, hiding during daylight hours, and coming out to raid and ambush at night.

Some of the villages were abandoned and others were fortified and garrisoned by the South. Many of them, torn by the fortunes of war, had been left undefended. Here the peasants were slaves on their own land, forced to grow food for a hidden army-in-residence, and in danger of being shot at by the southern government for doing so.

You could just about tell the loyalties of a given village, though, by the booby traps and mines. The higher the "accident ratio," the likelier it was that the locals were in sympathy with the northerners. These troops were no match for Americans in open combat, and the ARVN could be depended upon to keep them in check—provided that American artillery and air support could be called in.

The NVA were building up for something, and were lying low, but they could be rousted out and brought to combat, if you could find them. In the meantime, they were raiding and setting mines and booby traps that were killing GIs and civilians—and we were determined to fight fire with fire.

The GIs had learned, even if their commanders hadn't, to spot hostile settlements; you could tell, just from the way the infantry carried themselves, what they thought about a particular village. One morning, a couple of days after we joined 3d Platoon, I spotted a line of approximately one hundred infantrymen waiting outside a hootch. This was unnatural conduct in a hot zone, so I asked the Apostle's TC what was going on.

"They've got a brand-new CO," he said. "And he told them yesterday that the next man who torched a thatch would get a fifty-dollar fine. They're just waiting to pay their fines in advance."

"Well," I said, "what the hell, the place ain't occupied, and every burned roof is one more wet, cold NVA."

The tanks weren't having to engage in much heavy combat just then; most of our work was setting counter mines and traps to keep the enemy off balance. For example, we knew that the hostiles were in the habit of poking around our campsites, so we arranged a few deadly surprises for them. A C-ration can is the perfect size container for an M26 frag. If the pin is pulled and a can is put down over the grenade, the next yokel that picks up the can had better have fast reflexes.

On one occasion, I left what looked like a forgotten case

of demolitions material behind when we broke camp, and the NVA came out of hiding to examine it before we even got clear of the hamlet. As a matter of fact, that crate did contain demolitions material, along with a lot of scrap metal—and an antimotion trigger.

Asians can be as sloppy and forgetful with military equipment as anybody else. We were forever finding lost magazines for AK47s lying around. It wasn't difficult to pull a few bullets and replace the powder with C4, then load some of these back into a magazine, which could be left in a very conspicuous place.

By the time we'd worked our way down to the southern end of the plain, the Executioner's crew was dog-damn-tired and ready for a break. But Captain Biggio had been called for a two-platoon sweep, so we went for one last run before ol' Zippo rotated out. Black and the Widow-maker met us just north of Bong Son, and the two tanks worked their way over the coastal hills and down to the beach, linking up with the main body.

Just as Black and I were walking over to the command track for a briefing, a medevac dropped in. The company medic rushed over to the chopper and threw in a small bandaged package and the bird took off—fast.

"What the hell, Pete?" I asked the medic.

"You know how we always have to remind the ground-pounders not to let their legs dangle over the sides of the tanks?" Without waiting for an answer, he went on. "One Pfc., only a week in-country, hadn't listened. When Apache, over there, backed up and turned sharply, the man's legs got sucked into the sprocket and pinched off. I snapped on two tourniquets and dressings, and shot the morphine to him. There was a chopper handy, and we heaved him on board. He kept saying over and over, 'They warned me, they sure did.' "

"Well, what was that little package?" Black wanted to know.

"The legs," Pete said. "The base surgeon radioed in and said, 'Send the legs. There's a chance,' so we called a second chopper to pick them up."

"I know they can do miracles," Black said, "but that's kinda far out. . . . We better go get briefed. The Old Man's giving us that 'come-here-you' look."

In our briefing, we were told that the idea was to flush out an NVA unit known to be in the area. Each tank had a squad of ground troops assigned to it, and we were to cover open country as rapidly as possible, concentrating on individual hamlets to try and take enemy units by surprise. I could have told them it wouldn't work, that you have to send the grunts in at midnight. But who listens to an E5 anyway?

There were four tanks ahead of us, each loaded with infantry, and we were following exactly in their tracks. For once, I didn't have to worry about mines—Whamboom! . . . The echoing concussion seemed to go on forever, but eventually I got the ninety fired, Smitty got a reload, and Roman, switching over to manual, got a decent pattern going. Our electrical system was dead, the engine was stalled, and the turret had to be cranked manually. Roman fired the gun with a hellbox, while I swung the cupola .50, hashing up as much real estate as possible, until the platoon could arrive.

We couldn't see through the cloud of dust and smoke that surrounded us, and we knew better than to fire forward, because that was from where help would come. There was an awful, throbbing ache in my gut, and I was having trouble with coordination. But I couldn't take time for it—Kennet was screaming in the driver's seat that he was burning. That didn't make sense—there was no smoke down there. Leaving Sanchez to hold the turret, I dove down to see what was wrong.

The smoke outside was thinning and three tanks, flanked by their infantry, moved into place around us as we jerked Kennet from the driver's box. He was covered with battery acid, his skin turning red. Sanchez and I threw him in a fairly deep section of rice paddy, sudsing him up and down for a while; then we stripped him naked and poured as much water over him as we could.

By the time the associated sniping was suppressed, I had stopped vibrating and could function effectively again. None of us really required a medevac, and the rest of the crews volunteered to help get the Executioner out—after all, the ol' girl was our home. We figured that the mine must have been a tilt-rod fuse; the dozer tank rode lower than other hulls, so we had set off a charge that other machines had ridden over with impunity.

The bottom of the hull was slightly bent, the transmission control rods were spaghetti, and the largest piece left of the six 100-amp batteries was about the size of my fist. Nothing else was seriously damaged, though, so we hooked up the tow cables to another tank and got the hell out of there.

After a thorough exam at the Air Cav field hospital, the surgeon advised me: "Basically, there isn't anything I can do. You're just loosened up inside—the ligaments that hold your organs in place are weakened. All I can do is prescribe pain killers and tell you not to run over any more mines. The same goes for the rest of your crew, of course. Keep your man, Kennet, out of the sun for a few weeks; he got the equivalent of a very bad sunburn from the acid. It's a good thing you men got him into that paddy as fast as you did."

Even with company maintenance helping, it took us the better part of a week to get the tank rehabilitated and running. We weren't hurrying; our orders were to move slowly and take it easy—all of us were in some sort of pain most of the time. Even though it was almost time to rotate out, I was damned if I would leave a wreck behind me. Besides, I was thinking, why not extend and take the last six months of my enlistment over here?

That way, I could take discharge in Thailand. I'd always liked sailing, as well as doing mechanical work, and with five thousand saved, I could buy a small coastal motor junk, and set up as a seagoing mechanic/trader. After the war was over, I reasoned, this place would have an economic boom, just like South Korea—and a smart man could get rich here.

The next day I was going to have to tell the Old Man whether or not he would have to find another dozer sergeant. But at that moment the afternoon sun was a hair too hot; I'd been lying out on the tank's steel deck, so I edged over to get into the shade of the coconut palm overhead. Half asleep, I gazed up at the feathery leaves outlined against an almost metallic-blue sky, and saw with horror that one coconut was falling faster than my reflexes could get me out of there.

Whomp! It fell right on my chest, aggravating the mine injury.

"Sarge, are you okay?" Kennet asked, jumping out of the canvas chair where he'd been resting.

Taking stock and deciding all my parts were still in place and functioning, I replied, "After a fashion, I guess. . . . But you're gonna have to break in a new tank commander. Zippo's gettin' outta here."

With Kennet's help, I hobbled over to the command bunker.

"I changed my mind, Captain. When a coconut falls on your chest, the gods are telling you to get out."

"That's impossible," he said.

"Oh, I saw it happen, sir," Kennet put in. "And the coconut is still lying on the turret."

Biggio very seldom smiled, but that wintery grin of his split his face as he shook my hand. "You did a hell of a job for us, Sarge, and there'll be some paperwork following you home. Good luck."

And home was another story.

APPENDIX

Tank Company Organization

Company Commander.	In command of the company; has own tank, and jeep with driver.
Executive Officer.	Second in command; handles operational detail work; has own tank (dozer), and jeep with driver.
First Sergeant.	Has own jeep with driver.
Company Clerk.	Works directly under first sergeant; keeps records.
Supply Sergeant.	Has clerk and driver.

Mess Section.	Consists of five cooks and one driver.
Armorer.	Repair maintenance technician; has one driver.
Motor Sergeant.	Head of five mechanics.
Ammunition Sergeant.	Has driver and two helpers.

This is the ideal Table of Organization—found only on paper at Division Headquarters. In reality the understaffed HQ section works its tail off keeping the combat crews fed and fueled. In A Company, all clerks, mechanics, and some cooks were cross-trained as armor crewmen, and any Pfc. found missing at reveille could be assumed to have been nabbed by a departing line platoon. (A platoon leader once seriously considered hiring Montagnards as loaders.)

Tank Platoon Organization

Numbering system.	Each tank's personal number consists of the platoon number, followed by the vehicle number. There is no number one; instead, the number six is used as the universal "command" number.
	Platoon leader: 3-6
	Company CO: 6
	Battalion CO: Big 6
Heavy Section.	Platoon leader & command tank: 3-6
	Line tank: 3-2
	Line tank: 3-3

| Light Section. | Platoon Sergeant & auxiliary command tank: | 3-4 |
| | Line tank: | 3-5 |

Tank Crew Titles and Responsibilities

Tank Commander.	The boss; he is responsible for the vehicle, its maintenance, and performance in battle, and is also the most likely to be killed in action.
Gunner.	Normally in control of main weapons. His function in Vietnam was as spare tank commander.
Loader.	Responsible for feeding all weapons and keeping supplies stocked.
Driver.	Drives tank and maintains engine, tracks, and electrical system.

DEPARTMENT OF THE ARMY

THIS IS TO CERTIFY THAT
THE

VALOROUS UNIT AWARD

HAS BEEN AWARDED TO THE

COMPANY A, 1ST BATTALION, 69TH ARMOR, 4TH INFANTRY DIVISION

FOR
EXTRAORDINARY HEROISM IN MILITARY
OPERATIONS AGAINST AN ARMED ENEMY.

IN THE REPUBLIC OF VIETNAM – 30 MAY 1967 TO 3 JULY 1967

GIVEN UNDER MY HAND IN THE CITY OF WASHINGTON
THIS   16TH   DAY OF   APRIL   1970

Stanley R. Resor

SECRETARY OF THE ARMY

DEPARTMENT OF THE ARMY
Headquarters, United States Army Vietnam
APO San Francisco 96375

GENERAL ORDERS   16 April 1970
NUMBER 878

AWARD OF THE VALOROUS UNIT AWARD

TC 439. The following AWARD is announced.

By direction of the Secretary of the Army, under the provisions of paragraph 202.1g(2), AR 672-5-1, the Valorous Unit Award is awarded to the following named unit of the United States Army for extraordinary heroism while engaged in military operations during the period indicated:

The citation reads as follows:

COMPANY A, 1ST BATTALION, 69TH ARMOR, 4TH IN-FANTRY DIVISION distinguished itself by extraordinary heroism while engaged in military operations during the period 30 May 1967 to 3 July 1967, in Binh Dinh Province, Republic of Vietnam. While in support of the 1st Cavalry Division (Airmobile), unit personnel participated in numerous tank-infantry assaults on well entrenched and heavily armed North Vietnamese Army and Viet Cong forces. Using the shock effect of armor to the fullest, they aggressively engaged the enemy with 90mm guns, coaxial machineguns and, often times due to the close quarter fighting, utilized hand grenades to dislodge the enemy from his well fortified positions. Demonstrating great determination and a remarkable grasp of the tactical situation, the men of COMPANY A, 1ST BATTALION, 69TH ARMOR, 4TH IN-FANTRY DIVISION skillfully located hostile emplacements and ably supported ground assault troops by delivering accurate and intense fire upon the enemy. Frequently during the heat of battle, tank crewmen employed their vehicles as shields, and despite intense enemy fire, they courageously dismounted their vehicles to assist wounded comrades and evacuate them from the battle zone. Their brave and selfless actions saved many lives and won the respect and admiration of those with whom they served. The men of COMPANY A, 1ST BATTALION, 69TH ARMOR, 4TH INFANTRY DIVISION displayed extraordinary heroism and devotion to duty which are in keeping with the highest traditions of the military service and reflect distinct credit upon themselves and the Armed Forces of the United States.

GLOSSARY

ACAV An M113 armored personnel carrier equipped with a shielded .50 caliber machine gun and two 7.62mm M60 machine guns.

AP Armor-piercing ammunition.

APC Armored personnel carrier.

ARA Aerial rocket artillery—a Huey carrying 2.75-inch rockets.

ARVN Army of the Republic of Vietnam.

AUXILIARY WEAPONS Lethal devices carried and used by tankers, but not mounted on the vehicle. The .45 automatic (seven shot, Colt pistol); M3 grease gun (thirty shot, .45 cal. submachine gun); 5.56mm M16 rifle; Car-16 (short version of the M16); M79 (single shot 40mm grenade gun); M60 LMG (7.62mm light machine gun, .30 cal.).

AVLB Armored Vehicle-laid Bridge.

B40 Older version of the RPG (antitank rocket).

BACK-SCRATCHING Removing hostiles who have boarded another tank, by firing light-caliber weapons at its buttoned-up turret.

BANK SHOT Shooting a delayed exploding shell to cause a deliberate ricochet, thus allowing tanks to shoot around corners.

BLOCS Individual tread sections (blocks).

BULLET STABBER Tanker vernacular for a loader—always the starting slot for a new man.

BUSTLE RACK A pipe framework in which noncritical supplies (bedrolls, C rations, and beer) were carried—attached to the rear of the turret.

BUTTON UP To shut and lock all hatches.

C4 White, putty-like, moldable explosive.

CANNISTER Can-shaped projectile containing 1280 metal cylinders.

CAN OPENER Euphemism for bulldozer tank.

CLAYMORE A directional mine that can fill a fan-shaped area with shrapnel.

CO Commanding officer.

CO-AX An M73, 7.62mm (30 cal.) machine gun mounted coaxially or parallel with the main gun, using the same sights.

COMMAND TANK Tank with extra radio capability, allowing communication with several levels of command.

COMMO Abbreviation for communication.

COMMO TRACK An M113 armored personnel carrier modified to carry radios; used as a mobile headquarters.

DEUCE-AND-A-HALF A 2½-ton military all-wheel-drive truck.

DONKEY SIGHT A primitive metal sight mounted for quick pointing—not for precision work.

DOOR GUNNER An infantryman who mans an M60 machine gun in a slick.

DOZER TANK A command tank with an extra 4,000-pound bulldozer kit that turns it into an extremely powerful, earth-moving machine, as well as a fighting vehicle.

DRAGON SHIP A DC-3 equipped with three Gatling guns.

EOD TEAM Explosive ordnance disposal.

FIFTY CALIBER .50 caliber Browning machine gun.

FLECHETTE Can-shaped projectile containing 8,000 steel darts.

FOOT-POUNDER Infantryman (slang).

FOOT-SLOGGER Infantryman (slang).

FRAG Hand grenade.

GP General purpose.

GREASE GUN M3 submachine gun (.45 caliber).

GREEN BEANIE Green Beret (slang).

GROUND-POUNDER Infantryman (slang).

H.E. High explosive.

HEAT Antitank high explosive (shaped charge).

H.E.P. High explosive plastic (C4).

H&I Harassment and interdiction—random night shots designed to keep the enemy off balance.

HQ Headquarters.

HUEY HU-1B helicopter.

HULL The lower part of the tank; holds the driver, controls, spare ammunition, batteries, fuel, and engine.

IG Inspector General.

IR Infrared.

KIA Killed in action.

KLICK Kilometer (slang).

LAAGER A Boer term for a circular defensive formation.

LCM Landing craft—medium.

LCVP Landing craft for vehicles and personnel.

LMG Light machine gun.

LRRP Long range reconnaissance patrol.

LURP Long range reconnaissance patrol (slang).

LZ Landing zone.

MEDEVAC A helicopter carrying EMT (emergency medical treatment) gear and medics, used for evacuation out of a combat zone—armed only with door gunners.

MG Machine gun.

MONTAGNARD The hill people of Vietnam.

MP Military police.

GLOSSARY

NCO Noncommissioned officer.

NCOIC Noncommissioned officer in charge.

NINETY Ninety millimeter long gun used as main armament on the M48 series of main battle tanks. Originally designed as an antiaircraft weapon, it has an extremely flat trajectory. As a direct-fire weapon, it has a range of forty four hundred yards; as an artillery piece, it can reach eight miles.

NVA North Vietnamese Army.

OCS Officers' Candidate School.

OVERRIDE The tank commander's personal control; mounted at the extreme right of the turret, it allows the TC to operate all the weapons from his position.

PARACHUTE FLARE A bright illuminating pyrotechnic, consisting of a small rocket and a parachute.

PB Patrol boat.

PC Personnel carrier.

PLASTIQUE Moldable plastic explosive.

PT76 Russian amphibious tank.

PUFF Popular forces (Montagnards).

RECON Reconnaissance.

REPPLE-DEPPLE Replacement depot—handles transfer of troops in and out of division-size units.

RHADÉ Tribe of Montagnards.

SCOUT TRACK An ACAV operated by Battalion Recon Platoon.

SF Special Forces (Green Berets).

SIX-BY 6×6—same as deuce-and-a-half.

SLICK A Huey helicopter, unarmed except for door gunners—also know as a skin ship.

SPONSON BOX Tool box on tank fender.

TANKER'S GRENADE Two pounds of TNT wrapped with barbed wire and/or sections of chain.

TC Tank commander.

TOP First sergeant.

TRIP FLARE Illuminating pyrotechnics designed to indicate enemy's location—triggered by a trip wire.

TURRET The upper part of a tank; contains the commander, loader, gunner, and all the weapons and communications gear.

VC   Vietcong.

VTR   Tank retriever.

WP   White phosphorus.

XENON SEARCHLIGHT   Seventy-five million candlepower, white-and-infrared searchlight, mounted on all tanks. In an emergency, its power can be doubled for short periods of time.

INDEX

INDEX

INDEX